The Secret Language of Influence

Master the One Skill
Every Sales Pro Needs

DAN SEIDMAN

AMACOM AMERICAN MANAGEMENT ASSOCIATION
New York · Atlanta · Brussels · Chicago · Mexico City
San Francisco · Shanghai · Tokyo · Toronto · Washington, D.C.

This publication is designed to provide accurate and authoritative information in regard to the subject matter covered. It is sold with the understanding that the publisher is not engaged in rendering legal, accounting, or other professional service. If legal advice or other expert assistance is required, the services of a competent professional person should be sought.

Library of Congress Cataloging-in-Publication Data

Seidman, Dan.
The secret language of influence : master the one skill every sales pro needs / Dan Seidman.
   p. cm.
Includes bibliographical references and index.
ISBN 978-0-8144-1726-3 — ISBN 0-8144-1726-4 1. Selling. 2. Consumer behavior. 3. Persuasion (Psychology) I. Title.
HF5438.25.S43574 2012
658.85—dc23

                                                                          2011051773

About AMA
American Management Association (www.amanet.org) is a world leader in talent development, advancing the skills of individuals to drive business success. Our mission is to support the goals of individuals and organizations through a complete range of products and services, including classroom and virtual seminars, webcasts, webinars, podcasts, conferences, corporate and government solutions, business books and research. AMA's approach to improving performance combines experiential learning—learning through doing—with opportunities for ongoing professional growth at every step of one's career journey.

Printing number
10 9 8 7 6 5 4

DEDICATION

How likely is this? A sales trainer is introduced to a leadership trainer (who also happens to have a stellar track record in selling—with Shell Oil). Her training products have produced over $50 million in sales, including over 4 million participant's guides. She likes him enough to fall in love at first sight (well, one of us did).

It took six months, and I close her, got the big YES to the big question, "Will you marry me?" And now she is my most trusted adviser as we work together to upgrade and redesign existing sales training programs.

How blessed can a guy get? You can even read about our first night together on page 98.

Next, my kids give me great joy. They keep me sane by increasing the laughter in our household. And by making me proud of their hard work at school, in sports, and with their solid friendships. Thanks, Josh, Abbie, and Bekah for loving me unconditionally. Everyone needs people like that to count on.

Finally, this book has to be dedicated to you—a pro committed to our profession. You know that our time on this planet is first about relationships. This is why selling is such a rich career. We get a wide, often wild variety of people to interact with every day.

You are my partner in this profession. You made a great decision to buy *The Secret Language of Influence*. When you finish this book and apply the ideas, you will find yourself in a better place than before we met. And that makes for a great relationship.

I am here for you.

ABOUT THE AUTHOR

Dan Seidman, CEO of Got Influence? is recognized as "One of the Top Sales Coaches in America" by *Ultimate Selling Power.*

His *Secret Language of Influence* program is a unique keynote and training experience that is designed to improve persuasion skills for executives, managers, and sales professionals. This program has been offered to major organizations like *Million Dollar Roundtable,* the premier event for this planet's top financial services pros.

Dan is a World Masters' athlete with three gold medals playing on the U.S. basketball team. World Masters' sports are the Olympics for athletes over thirty-five.

Dan has authored five books, including the 900-page encyclopedia of best practices *Ultimate Guide to Sales Training* (Pfeiffer, 2012).

He is the designer of the global sales training program for the American Society for Training & Development which has 74,000 members worldwide.

Dan lives in Barrington, Illinois, with his Princess Bride, Wendy, and son, Joshua. Twin girls were recently discovered at his residence. They're being called Abigail and Rebekah.

You can find Dan at www.GotInfluenceInc.com.

CONTENTS

PREFACE: Great Persuasion Skills Are Invisible

Denise was a classic rags-to-riches story, having advanced from a secretarial position to become CEO of her own promotion products firm, where her professional highlight was working on a marketing campaign with basketball legend Michael Jordan. Because she had taken an unusual career path (with zero formal training in selling skills), she was meeting with me to discuss whether to implement sales coaching to further build her business.

I had two meetings with Denise to persuade her that a two-year training program would help her attain her business growth goals. The second call was to pick up the check that proved her commitment to the class. As she handed it to me I asked, "Denise, what's the real reason you want to do this training? I mean, two years is a serious obligation for someone who is busy, running a successful business."

Her answer was a total surprise and still gives me chills when I replay it in my mind. She said, "Dan, I want to be able to do exactly what you did with me. I don't know what you did, but I want to know how to do it. How did you influence me to say *yes*?"

As you read through the stories and strategies contained within this book, you will come to understand that great selling is invisible.

Influence occurs at a level just below the buyer's awareness. That's important because today's buyer is savvy—and too familiar with traditional selling techniques. When you begin to customize dialogues, tailoring your words to the person you are dealing with, you will discover a way to have a casual, comfortable, and customized conversation that gives both you and the buyer a unique decision-making experience.

The Secret Language of Influence was written so that you could learn how decision makers filter and process their experience in order to make a decision. This is psychologically sound information that psychologists have used for decades to help patients change their minds and their behavior.

And isn't that our job with buyers? To help them change products and services, change vendors, change their minds?

Pay close attention to your improvement in language skills as you begin to match your word choices to the exact phrases your buyers need to hear. Let's just say you are beginning to speak fluently in the buyer's dialect.

How do you identify the other person's dialect? You test people. You test your buyers overtly, with specific questions. For example, you might ask, "Why is having X [your product or service offering] important for you?" As you'll see in Chapter 2, depending on the answer, you'll know whether your dialogue with the buyer is going to be about sharing benefits or, conversely, addressing problems.

You can also test buyers covertly, just by attending to their word choices or speed of talking. For example, imagine that a prospect says, "It looks like we need to handle this matter fairly fast. I saw the data and decided to take care of it myself." You could assume that this buyer processes information visually (her word choices are "looks like" and "saw") and that she is fairly proactive rather than reactive to a situation (note the buyer's "self-starter" language). Identify a buyer's dialect and you'll also learn to pay attention to your own.

In the final part of this book you'll read about an assessment you can take to deepen your understanding of the value of these concepts and to identify your own motivation and decision-making strategies. This Model of Sales Excellence assessment tool is incredibly powerful for three reasons:

- You'll have a document that shows you exactly how you are like your buyer. Or, if you are different from your buyers, it will help you understand how to adjust your approach to match their dialect.

- You can significantly deepen the sales training ideas taught here when you realize this book isn't a conceptual document but rather a map to getting inside the world of your buyers' brains.

› Your company can actually use this tool to model its best reps, in order to hire the exact sales professional that is most likely to succeed in your business.

Wait to the end or skip right now to www.ModelofSalesExcellence.com for white papers and additional details.

One thing you should know is that these strategies are organic. By that I mean that they work in both your personal and professional lives. This is key to attaining great influence skills because you can actually practice what you learn here until you perfect the techniques. This can't be done in sales training, because pure selling techniques must be practiced in the classroom before you begin to engage buyers.

Starting today, however, you can use your newly adopted influence strategies at home, with friends, and in the workplace. That's a big bonus for a serious learner like you!

So let's get started on our journey toward greater influence and persuasion power.

Dan Seidman
Barrington, IL
April 2012

PART ONE

Influencing Others

I confess. . . . This book was originally going to be titled:

Buyers Are Babies
How to Change Them Before
They Stink Up Your Sales

My editor said it was the worst book title he'd read in more than three decades of publishing. I thought the baby metaphor was cute, but he convinced me not to embarrass myself (and ruin book sales).

So you'll have to settle for *The Secret Language of Influence,* and in the chapters of Part 1, you'll learn how to influence other people by speaking their dialect in several ways.

You'll start with a wild strategy you've used at home, but never recognized as a sales technique. Along the way, you'll discover exactly when your dialogue should address benefits and when you need to sell with pain. You'll get some quick, cool language tips, and you'll learn about the use of humor, emotion, and a very potent and psychologically sound strategy for handling objections.

As you absorb the information and think about how you can use it during your selling day, you'll begin to increase your ability to influence in amazing new ways.

CHAPTER 1

Breaking Buyers' Patterns

THE "MOST ELUSIVE PROSPECT" . . . I'm selling for a company in Chicago. When I'm not on the road, I'm pounding the phones at my desk, generating leads. Today, in fact, I'm breezing through my contact manager when I stop and stare at the notes section of one record.

There's the date and time of the last call, and next to these notes are the letters "lvm," short for "left voice mail." Below this note is a string of identical calls going back three years. We have "left voice mail" messages for this woman forty-six times!

Now, what would you do with a prospect like that?

"What is there to lose?" I think, so I dial and—surprise—get her voice mail. I wait for the beep and leave a message.

"Congratulations! This is Dan Seidman of corporate recruiting. You have earned our company's prestigious Most Elusive Prospect Award. We have called you forty-six times—today makes forty-seven—and you have never returned a single call. I just wanted you to know that nobody in our entire database, with thousands of companies, has ever ignored us as frequently as you. Thanks for not calling. And congratulations on your award."

I hang up.

And what do you think happens? Ninety minutes later the woman calls me! And I get an earful. "You stupid jerk! I don't have to return anybody's calls, ever. How rude to leave me that message. Don't ever call our company again. You're a jerk."

I manage to get a word in—"Wow, I had no idea you'd be upset. I'm so sorry"—and *bang!* She hangs up the phone.

Oh, man, what did I do? Well, at least she called me and not my VP of sales.

Moments later, the phone rings again. It's her! She proceeds to tell me how awful she feels popping off at me like that. And, actually, my message was pretty funny. And, yes, she does use services like ours. Then she asks if I would please come in to see her next week, to talk about our offerings

Yes, she became a client and no, my VP never did hear about my cold-calling strategy.

You're wondering, What happened here? The story I just told illustrates what's called, in psychology, a *pattern interrupt.* Its roots are fascinating, and the strategy is useful as you learn to better influence others.

The late Dr. Milton Erickson is considered one of the world's great psychologists. He perfected pattern interruption and other creative influence techniques to help patients work through problems that result from being stuck in a pattern of thinking or behavior. His ability to help patients change behavior—and to stop doing those things that are damaging to themselves and others and instead do things that are useful—is legendary.

And isn't influencing your buyers to change really the ultimate goal of selling?

As I mentioned in the book's preface, as sales professionals, we need to help prospects to change products and services—to change their minds. And as you probably know from experience, people often follow a well-worn path when encountering situations where discomfort occurs (a sales rep calling, for example). Dr. Erickson revealed how we can move them off this path and, by doing so, open up the possibility of different outcomes. In other words, we're going to break their tried-and-true patterns.

Learning to Respond in an Unexpected Way

So let's return to the example of selling: Sales pros encounter similar problems every day when prospects throw the same old objections at them: "We don't have money for this. . . . Let me think about it. . . . Call me in six months." But what if salespeople can learn to respond in an unexpected manner? They can break that bad dialogue and create a useful conversation that is more likely to end in a decision. But first, how did that jump from the world of psychology to the world of business occur?

The bridge between pure psychological counseling and related business applications was built by Richard Bandler and John Grinder, creators of *neuro-linguistic programming* (NLP), a technique used in psychotherapy and in organizational change management. Bandler and Grinder studied and then modeled Erickson's techniques. Bandler had some fantastic success experimenting with and testing the pattern interrupt technique on patients in mental hospitals. He decided to find extreme cases of antisocial behavior—people who had spent years institutionalized—and treat these individuals differently than traditionally trained doctors were taught. His results proved both astounding and at times humorous.

In one case, Bandler was called in to help treat a man who thought he was Jesus Christ. Here's a fellow who insisted he was someone he was not, in spite of counselors saying, "C'mon, man, you are not Jesus. What makes you think that?"

Bandler approached the man and asked him if he was Jesus Christ. The patient eyed him suspiciously but eventually replied that he was. Bandler left the room and returned some time later, again asking the man if he really was Jesus Christ.

"Yes, my son, what can I do for you?" was the man's reply. The psychologist left the room again. Soon he returned with two huge beams of wood, twelve-inch nails, and a big hammer.

The man asked, "What is this about?"

Bandler replied, "If you're Jesus Christ, you know what we're here for; we have come to crucify you."

The man looked at the size of the nails and quickly said, "You don't understand. I'm not really the Christ. I'm crazy. I just imagine I'm the Christ."

Pattern interrupt had penetrated a solid wall of defense. In that moment the man with the muddled mind was about to take the first important step in his healing process.

In another case, a patient had been in a catatonic trance for more than six years. Catatonia is a state where the person completely withdraws from the world. This individual had not spoken in six years. He'd wake up each day, dress, eat, and walk into the common area of the clinic where other patients played cards and table tennis, read books, and watched TV. But he would just stand against a wall and stare. All day, every day, the man had no connection with anyone or anything except his food. The man's family would visit and say, "Honey, please, we love you, come back to us." No response. Drugs did not work, nor did electric shock therapy (which, by the way, is still used today).

Then Bandler went to work: He brought in a red gas can filled with water and some nail polish remover (to add a distinct smell). He walked up to the catatonic patient and splashed this "gasoline" all over him.

No response.

Bandler stepped back, removed a small cardboard box from his pocket, and began to throw lighted matches at the man. Within moments, the patient exploded into a rage, screaming foul language at this man who was intending to set him on fire!

Wouldn't you do the same?

Again, pattern interrupt had broken down bad behavior and started the individual off on a path of new possibilities.

Applying Psychology in the Sales Environment

Okay, you're thinking, "This is interesting. But how can I use this strategy in my business life?" There are outstanding ways to apply this technique and other new influence strategies, described throughout this book, in every facet of your world—when leading, managing, or even having customer service conversations. For now, let's continue to focus on how to use pattern interrupt in a sales environment.

One of the biggest problems we face as sales professionals is that today's buyers are savvy and they know how to put us off, to get rid of us, by hauling out some standard responses that they've learned work. You know what they are: *We're happy with what we have now,* or *There's no money in the budget; call back in six months*—the kind of responses that get the acid sizzling in your stomach and the blood boiling in your brain.

We're done with that, as of right now, today. Let's get started.

Take your six most common objections. Every business has six objections that do the most damage to the salesperson's ability to close. (By the way, you'll get even more powerful and unique objection-handling techniques in Chapter 12.) For each objection, create an unexpected response. In essence, you are saying to the prospect, "I'm not going to play this game with you. It's not fun, and it's costing me income."

Here's an example I used with a money objection when I ran a search firm with a team of fifteen sales professionals:

Prospect: This is a tough time. We don't have money for this right now.

Dan: What floor are you on? *(pattern interrupt)*

Prospect: Huh? What floor? What do you mean?

Dan: Things are bad, that's rough. I just want to know what floor because when you throw yourself out the window, I'm wondering whether you'll die or just break some bones.

Prospect: Okay, okay. It's not that bad.

Dan: So you *are* spending money when you feel it's worth the investment?

You see, we're back in selling mode, having broken the pattern that this prospect has used to dump countless salespeople back onto the street.

A few years ago I even built pattern interrupt responses into a sales training program that I designed (actually redesigned to include the latest influence strategies) for a major financial services company. We logged over three dozen objections and I crafted one response that I call "my favorite response to any objection, ever!" The buyers in this case were senior citizens who sometimes said, "I'm too old to buy an annuity." The response: "We have sea turtles older than you as clients."

Say that with a big smile and the message to the prospect is clear: Please stop playing games, let's move on.

Now, you might be thinking, "I can't say something like that!" Well, the fact is, great sales professionals will say and do things that mediocre reps won't. And typical salespeople won't for several reasons:

- They don't have these strategies in their arsenal; they have never heard or experienced them.

- They haven't ever gotten so angry at getting jerked around by buyers that they'll try something different, something gutsy, to overcome that frustration.

- They are simply not serious enough about their sales career to take risks that might generate significant reward.

Funny thing is, all of us have probably used pattern interrupt on people in our personal lives but didn't recognize it as a potent psychological strategy. Have you ever dealt with a child throwing a tantrum (or observed someone else doing so)? When you pulled out a toy and tried to put it in the little one's hands, or pointed to a pretty bird, or cranked up some favorite music, you were using pattern interruption.

You can use pattern interrupt in sales situations, too, and have fun doing it. Decide today to create some unique responses to objections and tell your prospects that you won't play games.

CHAPTER 2

Toward Buyers and Away Buyers

LET'S TALK ABOUT MY BIG *BUT*. . . You're sitting with a good friend and the topic of vacations comes up. She says, "Hey, what's the greatest trip you could ever take, anywhere? Would you fly, drive, cruise on a ship? Picture the location in your mind—what would you do there? What are all the great things you'll do and experience?"

You respond, "I'd go to Tahiti, it's gorgeous!" She shakes her head and says, "Yeah, but it takes ten hours to get there. You'll be exhausted."

"That's okay," you say, "I'll just crash at the beach to catch up on sleep."

"But you'll probably fry in the sun and ruin the rest of the trip."

"I'm not stupid. I'll wear a good sunscreen."

"But you know that stuff is toxic, right? You're burning chemicals into your skin."

"I can buy some natural lotion."

"But do you know how expensive those 'organic' products are?"

And on it goes, as she plays the devil's advocate, protesting and disagreeing with every thought you think, until you want to scream.

How many times have you had just this type of conversation with your prospects? How many of them disagree and just want to talk about their big *buts* . . . ?

I first recognized this type of person from an incident in my younger days:

I'm twelve years old and fly into the house after school. "Mom, Dad, guess what I decided today? When I grow up, I'm gonna be a doctor!"

Mom is wonderful, always encouraging me. Her immediate response is, "Honey, that's great! Doctors are so well respected. You'll make good money, have a nice house and a wonderful spouse. I'm delighted you want to be a doctor."

How does Dad respond? "A doctor? *A doctor?*" he says. "Do you know how much money it costs to become a doctor? A fortune! Do you want to go to school for sixteen more years? And you'll be working with sick people all day. And there's malpractice insurance, and lawsuits, and long, long hours. Are you out of your mind? You want to be a doctor?"

Wow! What a contrast between Mom's and Dad's responses.

Psychologists would say that Dad is exhibiting a "polarity response." He moves away from other people's ideas. While the clinical terminology itself might be new to you, you have probably experienced it from others your whole life.

The real problem in selling is that prospects use the polarity response as well. Here, then, is a critical teaching moment for your sales life:

People either move toward ideas or away from them.

You'll learn how to deal with these prospects shortly. But first, examine your own behavior. Do you exhibit a polarity response to others? Are you always prefacing your responses with comments like "Yeah, but . . ." or "What if . . . ?"? Do you play the devil's advocate? Here's a quick quiz to reveal whether you move *toward* or *away* from the ideas of other people. It's also fun to try this set of questions on friends, coworkers, and family members, to further help you to identify these two types of people.

1. A friend describes a new business idea; you immediately:

   a. Point out some concerns he should address.

   b. Say, "Great! Go for it!"

2. You ask your significant other about buying a new car; your partner responds:

   a. I'm not sure; we're talking about $25,000, and big payments.

   b. Well, there are a lot of zero percent finance options. Let's check them out.

3. You tell the decision maker, "We can increase the productivity of your staff by 22 percent in sixty days." He replies:

   a. I'm not sure that's possible. We've tried a lot of things like this before that didn't work.

   b. That sounds impressive. How can you do that?

Where do you see yourself? Do you move toward or away from ideas?

Here's a specific application of the polarity response for salespeople today: *Benefits-oriented selling does not work well with prospects who "move away" from your ideas.*

One of the problems with pulling out a laundry list of benefits is that it tempts salespeople to talk too much. We hope that by reeling off a long list of goodies, one item might strike a chord and help sell the whole package. Therefore, all too often, benefits-based sellers don't know when to stop. It's like a mechanic saying, "I couldn't fix your brakes, so I made the horn louder."

However, let's look at the value of resistance from the buyer's perspective. It is not a bad thing to move away from ideas. People need to protect themselves from poor decisions. Buyers may feel a strong need to shelter their company's money, reputation, and future. They also want to guard their personal reputation, perhaps even their job, from being jeopardized by a bad decision.

So you'll need two different strategies, depending on whether you are selling a person who is drawn to benefits or resistant to them. (Notice that we've wandered into the concept of *flexibility* and its value to a salesperson. Flexibility is likely the most important influence strategy you can learn. Because it affects the dialogues you have with buyers throughout the sales process, you will use it more often than anything else you'll learn in this book.) Very simply, then, we are going to divide our whole world of potential customers into two categories:

To and *Away*

This simple approach covers people who move toward ideas (e.g., benefits and goals). And it covers those who move away from ideas (e.g., problem solvers). You can call them Mom and Dad, or sheep and goats, or whatever you choose.

You can change your sales approach (dialect) depending on whether you are presenting to someone who moves to or away from ideas. Let's look at the most effective ways to motivate each type of prospect.

The Buyer Who Moves <u>Toward</u> New Ideas

This is easy. It's probably what you have been doing for years. You offer features and benefits so that your buyers can understand what they will gain by doing business with you. Now, let's upgrade this approach to give it more impact.

It is extremely valuable to see that the benefits you offer are *personalized* to the buyer. Here are three contrasting statements to show how it's done:

1. "This equipment is faster than anything you have, and when you install it, you will be able to take on more business without increasing your labor costs." (Weak)

2. "This equipment is 40 percent faster than anything you have, and when you have it up and running, you will increase your revenue by $1,300 a week in this department." (Good)

3. "This equipment is 40 percent faster than anything you have, and when you have it up and running, you will increase your revenue

by $1,300 a week in this department. Ms. Prospect, are these numbers important enough to have an effect on how you are perceived as a decision maker within your company?" (Superior)

How's that last one for a gutsy comment to make to a potential client? The third example is both specific and personalized. Think about the best possible impact your product or service can have on that individual, not just the company.

The Buyer Who Moves <u>Away</u> from New Ideas

My selling skills used to be ugly and skinny. Sales superstars would kick sand in my face—and take my commissions. That hurt, a lot, and for a long time.

Then I learned that most of my pain was from butting heads with buyers.

Buyers develop a resistant mindset because they like to focus on trouble. Their mentality is oriented toward solving problems rather than attaining goals. So, with this type of buyer, your dialogue should focus on the problems your product or service can solve, rather than all the good things the individual buyer gets from it.

I learned to magnify buyer frustrations or consequences when I was selling at an executive search firm. Before that point of enlightenment, I was using traditional features/benefits selling. So were all of my competitors. We were like poorly trained parrots, all born from the same bad bloodline:

Me: Hello, this is Dan Seidman with Management Recruiters. I have a Xerox-trained sales executive, she has hit 150 percent of her quota the last three years, is the top rep out of twelve in this area. She's really sharp. She'll represent your company well.

Prospect (ready to begin with the objections): I'm fine, got plenty of people from my ads, am already interviewing plenty of candidates, and I don't want to pay fees to headhunters.

Now the verbal fencing match is engaged. And I'd make great follow-on comments like, "Why not take a top person from me and get rid of someone at the bottom of your team?" or, "Wouldn't it be worth your time to meet someone who can make you more money?" and so on.

It was the beginning of plain old ordinary selling. In other words, it was the beginning of an argument. In particular, I remember that favorite buyer blow-off: "Send me some literature and call me back in a few weeks."

Do these prospects ever answer the phone when you call them back? Me neither.

I got very angry at the frequency of rejection by these buyers. So I spoke with my friend Rich, who explained to me how people are motivated not always by benefits, but by a belief that their efforts are best spent solving problems. His observations underscore my point: You have to prepare two completely different conversations, based on which type of person you are speaking with.

So I took my phone script and rewrote it, inverting it from a focus on the benefits I offered to the problems I could solve. I will never forget the first time I used this new approach with a prospective client, a sales manager I'll call John. Here's how the conversation evolved:

Me: Hi, John, I heard you had an open territory. How's it going?

John: Well, I'm very busy interviewing people now. (*Notice he's setting me up to get off the phone with the "very busy" comment.*)

Me: Good, hope you find someone. So who's covering the open territory?

John: I am.

Me: In addition to managing your other people and all your other work?

John: Yes.

Me: Oh, no (*speaking tongue-in-cheek*). That's probably not taking too much extra time from your day?

John: No, it's not really affecting my days (*joking*). I just work into the evening.

Here, as the conversation relaxes and he begins to joke, emotions begin stirring. It is very important to develop questions for gaining rapport during these moments (as you'll learn in Chapter 11).

Me: Since you've been doing the work of this missing person, is your family okay with the extra hours you're putting in?

John (after a long pause): You know what? I haven't been home for dinner in two weeks. And my wife is a great cook!

He said those exact words. I remember them distinctly because I still get goose bumps remembering that moment. It was the moment I recognized that this conversation was unlike any I'd had in my sales career.

I continued, asking other problem-oriented questions: Do your competitors know that these accounts aren't being visited? ("Yes, I'm interviewing a few of them," John said.) Is the missing person costing the company much money? (His answer: "I know exactly how much revenue is missing each week the territory is uncovered.") Is this situation costing *you* money? ("Of course. I get paid partially based on my reps' performance.") The situation was being framed by the trauma he was experiencing.

The result: Five minutes into the phone call he asked me if I had anyone for him to see. Imagine that! I had not presented a product or service to him. I had not presented any benefits I could offer. There wasn't even a hint that I had a solution for his problem. But he knew one thing about me that was true: I knew his situation, his personal experience. So who was better qualified to help him—me, or a pushy competitor who's calling to "present" candidates for the job?

Let me share a few insights about teaching consequences to your prospects:

▸ You do a lot less talking.

▸ You don't have to be able to "handle objections" since you offer nothing to object to.

▸ You demonstrate that you know what the real trouble is. It is not a missing salesperson. It is all the aggravation—experienced corporately, financially, and most of all, personally by the individual—of dealing with problems that can be fixed with your product or service.

John became a client, but that wasn't the end of the story. Later, he called to tell me what happened after our initial phone call. He said our conversation had been so unusual that he told his wife about it at home later that evening (after eating leftovers, reheated for the third night in a row). He told her that while the choices between my service and a competitor's were fairly even, I had a much better understanding of the complete reality and the scope of the decision. And that's why he chose to do business with me.

This experience revolutionized my belief about my ability to sell. Here I was, so in sync with my buyer, *speaking his dialogue*, as it were, that I was able to create rapport, then agreement, as both of us worked toward the goal of solving his problems.

A Simple Three-Step Strategy

I now teach a simple strategy to help salespeople identify which of the two types of buyers they are dealing with and what language to use when talking to each.

We've defined the benefits buyer as someone who moves toward ideas. *To* people like goals, gains, good things. In contrast, the person who is motivated by a problem-solving mentality moves away from ideas. *Away* people focus on present and future problems. You may have heard salespeople talk about finding the prospect's "pain." This indicates a sales approach that assumes the buyer is an Away person.

Here is a three-step strategy to prepare you to sell to both types.

Step 1. Take a sheet of paper. Draw a line down the middle. Write "Benefits" at the top of the left side of the page and "Problems" on the right.

On the left side, list all the good things that customers gain from your product or service. You'll most often find this information in marketing literature or on your company website. On the right side, list all the problems your product or service solves.

It's easy now to look at each benefit and identify an "opposite" problem. For example, a brand-new car is prestigious (benefit) and contrasts with an older car that might be embarrassing to be seen driving (problem). Make sense? Now, craft a document that clearly lists language that is To and Away—that is, both benefits focused and problem oriented. This exercise is easy to do, and I suggest you share this concept with your sales team or a group of entrepreneurs at your next networking meeting.

Here's an example from the automotive industry, for selling a new car:

Benefits	Problems
Prestige of owning a new car	Can't take a client to lunch in my old car
Cool color	Old look says that I'm not successful
0–60 mph in eight seconds	Dangerous to merge in traffic
Rides and handles like a dream	Can feel every bump in the road
100,000-mile warranty	Surprised by what breaks down every month

You want to create as large a list as possible so that all the sales professionals can "find their voice" and use language they are most comfortable with.

Step 2. Take another sheet of paper and create a list of questions that evoke emotion related to each benefit or problem. This is where selling becomes fun. This is where you begin to generate those customized conversations.

Step 3. Get in front of your prospect and ask this question: Why is having X important for you? X refers to your product or service offering, or the specific criteria the buyer has related to this decision.

For example, if the buyer said she wanted to talk to you because her company needs a new computer system, then you want to feed that information back in the form of a question: Why is it important for you to replace your current system or buy a new one? (Or, put another way, what is important to you about a new computer system?) The answer reveals whether you are dealing with a To or an Away buyer.

KEY TIP: You may initially get a superficial response to your question, so I suggest you dig deeper, two or three times, once the buyer replies. Say, "Good, tell me a bit more about that," or ask, "How so?"

One type of response might be: "A new system would allow us to upgrade our software." (Tell me more.) Or the buyer might say, "Well, our clients aren't happy with the graphical quality of some of our marketing literature." (How so?)

Another response might sound like this: "In one instance, we spent more money than we made farming out a project to someone with better software. In another case the client just left us and hired its own in-house designer, outfitted with the best software and hardware available." This is an Away buyer who has just listed several problems that are going to influence decision making.

The buyer might even say, "A new system would keep our design team happy." (Tell me more.) "We sell our company by having the best benefits possible. The latest hardware and software is very attractive to potential hires." (How so?) Another possible response: "We have a great image in the marketplace and senior management is proud of the quality of people who work here and the products they produce." Listen carefully and you can discern that this person is clearly a To buyer who is focused on gaining several good things related to this decision.

▶   ▶   ▶

In summary, buyers are motivated by benefits (making them receptive to ideas) or by problems that need solving (moving them away from ideas proposed by other people). You can ask a simple question to identify the type of buyer you are speaking with: *What is important to you about X?* (where *X* represents your product or service offering or the specific criteria the buyer has related to this decision). Prepare a list of benefits your company offers as well as the problems you solve, and keep your discussions centered on the dialect of the buyer, either To or Away.

CHAPTER 3

Buyer Tortoises vs. Buyer Hares

ROCK, PAPER, SCISSORS . . . To further enhance my decision-making capabilities, I joined the World RPS Society. You remember the game you played as a kid where scissors cuts paper, paper smothers rock, rock smashes scissors.

My membership package included a very cool T-shirt with a great picture on it and this motto: SERVING THE NEEDS OF DECISION MAKERS SINCE 1918. I also got a copy of *The Official Rock Paper Scissors Strategy Guide* and a membership card with the title I selected (my first decision after joining): "Intergalactic Director of Member Acquisition."

Douglas Walker, managing director of the World RPS Society, knew that I'd be pointing lots of people in his direction. So he granted me that title when I called to interview him for this book.

The rock, paper, scissors game has shown up on the screen over the years. Sean Connery used it (and won) as James Bond in *You Only Live Twice.* It's made television appearances on *The Simpsons* and on *Seinfeld,* where Kramer and his "little person" friend Mickey display their inflexibility, every time they compete, by both only choosing rock.

When I asked him to share some decision-making stories from the business world, Walker told me about the Match of the Century.

Takashi Hashiyama is the founder and director of the Maspro Art Museum in Japan. He owns a significant collection of Impressionist art masterpieces and decided to sell off thirty-seven of them. But Hashiyama couldn't determine which auction house giant to engage—Christie's or Sotheby's.

The museum director resorted to a strategy he employs when he is stuck between choices—a game that's been in play throughout Japan since the 1700s: rock, paper, scissors. The outcome of the game would determine which auction house to hire.

Actually *they* would play. Christie's and Sotheby's would compete against each other. The price tag on this decision was significant. The sale on four pictures alone would total $17.8 million. Commission on this portion of the artwork amounted to more than $2 million. If you are a salesperson on this account, you are drooling down the front of your suit.

On a Thursday afternoon, each auction house was informed that it would have until Monday to choose its weapon. One organization did research over the weekend. The other was resigned to being involved in a random game of chance.

On Monday, each company sent a representative to Tokyo, where they made their selection, drew a picture, and handed it to the museum director. Christie's chose scissors, cutting up Sotheby's paper and shredding its shot at significant commissions on the artwork. Christie's had actually finalized its decision-making strategy after a conversation with the daughter of one of its executives. The girl suggested always starting with scissors. Rock is too obvious a choice. So an inexperienced opponent, assuming rock was coming, would take paper. This is just how Sotheby's lost the game and the sale.

When I finished compiling this crazy sales story it was clear to me that the difference between the winner and loser was obvious. The Christie's executive was proactive and aggressively pursued a solution to the situation. The other party represented Sotheby's poorly by sitting back, waiting for what life had to offer, and taking a loss as part of the program. This story illustrates the motivational pattern we want to identify next: proactive vs. reactive buyers.

Fast-Moving Seller Encounters the Slow-Moving Buyer

Proactive people are the classic self-starters that every employer is looking for when hiring kids out of college. They are fired up to go, to get things done.

Reactive buyers, in contrast, are content to analyze and wait. They often frustrate others because they are rarely in a hurry to make a decision.

I encountered the classic reactive buyer profile, in great numbers, when I made a presentation on the *Secret Language of Influence* at a meeting of the Casualty Actuarial Society. Actuaries spend their lives analyzing data for insurance companies about how long people live. I joked during the program that I had the latest statistics on the lifespan of actuaries: "You don't live any longer than the general population. But doing actuarial work makes it seem a lot longer." These are slow-moving business professionals.

On the selling front, buyers who are slow to move can be very difficult for the fast-moving sales professional. You can identify whether your buyers are proactive or reactive, not with a question, but by listening to specific verbal cues and by paying attention to their body language.

Proactive Buyers. These individuals are goal- or outcome-oriented, and their behavior reflects the desire to attain those goals. Their body language often reveals rather impatient individuals who fidget and move continually. Their language also shows continual movement, since they favor short sentences, active verbs, and strong wording. For instance, proactive buyers may say:

"We're going to take care of this quickly."

"This company is ready for change."

Reactive Buyers. These individuals respond to the behavior of others and external circumstances. They tend to come across as sedentary. Their language reveals a great deal of thought and processing, rather than action. Reactive buyers might make comments such as:

"Once we have all the details, we can start to put together a chart to identify which vendors we can begin talking to."

"Our leadership is pretty busy with a lot of decisions, so I'm going to get feedback from some of our executives, then will get back to you."

Language to Use to Motivate Proactive and Reactive Buyers

Encourage your proactive buyers to take the next step and move forward with their decision by saying:

"Let's do this."

"Good thing you can take care of this and move on to other projects."

Help your reactive buyers understand that they have done all the pre-work and analyses they need and can now decide. You can motivate them by saying, for example:

"You've done some great research."

"That's great that you have feedback from your executives on the value of our offering. It looks like that's just about everything you can do, so the next step in the process is to get it implemented."

When presenting to a group or team, you must blend language to cover each of these motivational types. An example might include a comment to a decision-making team like, "You've thought this through and carefully gathered plenty of data. That's a smart way to get to the point where you can make a decision. Let's get on this now, before circumstances change; let's not wait any longer."

▶ ▶ ▶

Proactive vs. reactive. Your challenge now is to see how quickly you can begin to recognize and respond to these two distinct types of decision-makers in your personal and professional life.

Doug Walker runs a Rock Paper Scissors international competition every fall. More than 1,000 people attend from around the world. You can read about these international events and see some very funny video clips at www.worldrps.com. (My favorite competitor from the past was the guy wearing aluminum foil on his head—to prevent others from reading his mind.)

> *KEY TIP: Join the World RPS Society. It's an inexpensive invest-ment and a valuable education in world-class decision making. (Plus, the T-shirt's unique.)* **Better yet, give the membership to your high-quality prospects.** *Isn't your job to help buyers quickly make the best and the wisest decision possible?*

CHAPTER 4

Buyers Who Like Proof vs. Buyers Who Don't

DOES YOUR HUSBAND THINK . . . ? I've been hired to coach the sales manager of an exclusive tennis club. We were discussing the New Year and how so many people are suddenly interested in getting into shape.

All of his reps were being taught to sell memberships by playing to the prospect's personal experience. They'd say to a woman, "Think how great you'll feel when you look in the mirror," or "Just think how happy you'll be to become a much better tennis player."

I said, "How about this question: 'Does your husband think you're fat?'"

"I can't ask that!" he said.

"No, you can't," I said, "but you could benefit by learning how different that question is." Then I explained how buyers have contrasting decision-making approaches:

▸ *Internal* types are motivated by their own inner feelings, experiences, and beliefs.

▶ *External* buyers make decisions based on outside resources, such as evidence, testimonials, and peer pressure.

I wish you could have seen the look on that sales manager's face as the truth of this concept crept past his ears into his brain. He was sharp enough to know there was something special about this approach to selling. "Cool idea. It makes so much sense," he said, and then he asked the question that you should be asking right about now: "But, how do I identify *which person is which type?*"

By now, it shouldn't surprise you that the answer is revealed by asking the person (i.e., your prospect) a specific question: "How do you know *you've* made a good decision?"

How the person answers will tip you off to the type of prospect you are selling. That prospect who was considering a membership to an exclusive tennis club might say:

"I'll just know it's right because I will feel better about myself." (This answer reveals internal motivation.)

or

"My friends will ask where I got the new body!" (External motivation is apparent.)

Psychologists have identified the value of addressing internally motivated and externally motivated people differently. This significant language strategy, in use for almost thirty years, can be extremely potent for your sales life.

Identifying the Internal Buyer

Internal buyers make decisions based on their own experience and internal standards. An internal person can have difficulty accepting other people's opinions, even good ones. These individuals also give little feedback to others, so you may be in the dark when trying to figure out what's going on in their mind. Evidence is only useful if it agrees with their opinions.

Identifying the External Buyer

External buyers need outside feedback; testimonials are powerful ways to influence them. Information from other sources is necessary to help them make decisions. Evidence is a potent, persuasive tool in motivating the external buyer.

Selling the Internal Buyer

Because most of us have been taught how critical it is to dump evidence in front of prospects in order to persuade them, we tend to assume that all prospects are external buyers. After all, the marketing department has developed some spectacular literature and dynamic websites just to influence prospects to contact you. "We're the biggest." "Surveys say we're the best." "We've been around the longest." "Here are pictures of our plants in China, Brazil, and Antarctica. . . ." You get the idea.

You want to keep from bludgeoning internal buyers with your materials. Instead, use language that this prospect will connect with: "You know what's best here. . . ." "I need your opinion. . . ." "Only you can decide what makes the most sense. . . ." You want to talk to that internal voice that tells these prospects they know what to do. In fact, that voice often questions the credibility of others with whom they don't agree. The safest thing to do here is to encourage internal buyers to make the call. If you discover that your evidence, your testimonials, and case studies agree with how this person thinks, then and only then can you bring it out to reinforce the buyer's personal knowledge and experience.

Selling the External Buyer

We can share our evidence with our external buyers, but we should reinforce that data with motivating words such as, "Think how highly others will view you when you decide to do this deal," or "Top authorities in your industry agree that our product . . ." The external buyer is persuaded by benchmarks and input from others.

▶ ▶ ▶

Remember, when presenting to a team or decision-making group, you have to speak to both types of buyers. So your language should reflect both

internal and external reference points. If you can ask your key question—
How do you know you've made a good decision?—and get feedback from
each individual, that would be a very potent way to speak to each person,
according to his "dialect."

Try this question on friends and family, too. You may be surprised by
how little you know about what motivates the people closest to you. Then,
after you've practiced on your peers (and not your prospects!), you are
ready to sell both types of buyers.

And, by the way, do you know which type you are—external or internal?

CHAPTER 5

Artist Buyers vs. Accountant Buyers

I JUST KNEW THERE WAS A QUESTION I FORGOT TO ASK. It's 1985. There's a guy (yours truly) who is new to selling recruiting services, but very well trained. He has one thing going for him—a great job-hunting candidate, Jane. Jane has three things going for her. She's a great salesperson, she's great looking, and her husband pitches for the Boston Red Sox. If you can't start a good conversation trying to place this woman into a sales job, you don't deserve to be in sales yourself.

Now the worst objection anyone can encounter in the search business occurs when your prospects say they won't pay fees to find salespeople. They can run an ad in the paper and get hundreds of responses. Why spend $12,000 on my services?

So, I'm in the middle of a phone pitch, presenting Jane to a magazine publisher I found in the Yellow Pages, and the guy says, "She sounds perfect. I'd pay your fee, if we hire her." I had a few more questions I was trained to ask about: the target audience, percentage of outside sales vs.

phone work, details on the company benefits package, and so on. But I stopped, skipped the rest of my homework, and set up the interview.

Within minutes of the completion of Jane's interview, the decision maker called me and spoke the words a recruiter lives for and loves to hear: "She's fantastic. She's perfect for the job. And hot." (Well, that last comment was a little awkward.) Then he said, "I'll pay her asking salary."

I told him that I'd call him as soon as I got her phone call and feedback on the interview.

Fifteen minutes later my phone rings.

"I can't believe you sent me there!" Jane screams at me.

It was a men's magazine. Soft porn. The title of the publication didn't give a hint. I had no idea where I was sending her. Hence the awkward "She's hot" comment. That was important to the buyer.

If I had finished asking the questions my selling system dictated, I would have avoided an embarrassing (but memorable) sales experience.

Jane cooled down and was pretty good-natured about it. We had some laughs later, but it was nothing compared to the laughs in the Red Sox clubhouse when the story worked its way over there, via her husband.

I learned then and there to follow the selling system, the success model that had been developed years before I arrived.

This chapter's teaching focuses on helping you to identify the difference between people who follow a methodology and those who are creative and love to wing it through life. In psychology, these types are referred to as Options and Procedures. I like to use the analogy that Option types are like artists. Procedures types are like accountants.

An artist is free-thinking and loves to build by breaking or ignoring the rules. Some high-level sales jobs require a great deal of mental flexibility and the selling pro has to have Options available if he wants to accomplish his goal of closing the sale. A high-level negotiated product or service sale is a good example of the need for flexibility.

In contrast, an accountant has to follow an exact system in order to create work that can be interpreted by others needing the information. Anyone picking up a financial spreadsheet from anywhere can quickly analyze the data, because the financial services industry long ago set standards, formulas regarding how to structure numbers. In high-volume phone selling, a system is a preferred strategy for gaining more cus-tomers. The caller has a specific set of words to present; she'll then ask closing questions and offer regulated responses to objections and other forms of resistance.

Companies can significantly increase their hiring of top sales perform-ers by modeling the best existing sales pros in the firm (see the Modelof SalesExcellence.com website). Data on phone salespeople show that scripted callers achieve three times the success as those who wing it on the phone. And while different industries and sales situations can require a variety of selling types, most successful sales professionals take a system-atic approach to their selling. This helps them know where they are in the sales process. Flexibility comes into play when handling a variety of objec-tions and surprises. Bottom line: Procedure-oriented sales reps tend to have an advantage in the profession.

So we can see some of the application of Options and Procedures to sales professionals. What about its use in identifying and dealing with buyers?

First, let's understand that the Options buyer is going to select your solution when it addresses the buyer's need to creatively solve the problem presented. The Procedures person will have a preference for solutions that show how you can methodically solve the issues at hand.

Just as we did with To and Away buyers (see Chapter 2), we want to pre-pare some language choices prior to encountering each type of buyer. Once again, start by creating a chart with headings: Options buyers in the left col-umn and Procedures buyers in the right.

Options	Procedures
Alternatives	Exact method
Flexibility	Proven way to do this job/task
Variety	Follow these steps
Choices	Systematically work through it

Again, the larger the list you can create, the easier it will be to land on some language you are most comfortable with.

Using a "Reason Filter"

So now we need to be able to identify which buyer is in front of us (or on the phone).

Your Options vs. Procedures identifier question is: "Why did you choose to X?"

X refers to the purchase the buyer is making, the car the person drives, or the job someone has chosen. The answer in the third example—job choice—gives you insight into how people engage in their daily workload. This is also known as the "reason filter," because it explains whether the person chooses to work in a structured role or a creative role. Therefore, you hear a response that reveals Options or Procedures.

Now, as an example, let's say the buyer is looking for a high-end sound system to go with her new fifty-five-inch flat panel TV. This woman answers your question and tells you why she chose to purchase a fifty-five-inch TV. Options people will list a variety of reasons or criteria for their decision. This reflects a free-thinking approach to decision making. Procedures people will describe a series of events or decisions that helped them arrive at the decision. That series represents to them a systematic way to determine what to do.

This buyer might say, "The right sound system would connect perfectly with my TV and I wouldn't need to figure out different ways to get them working together." This is a Procedures buyer. She has clearly stated she wants something to fit and wants to avoid a creative solution to getting everything functioning.

Or, she might instead respond by saying this: "The right sound system would give me the flexibility to play a variety of media, including DVDs, CDs, MP3, or even hook up my video recorder right away to view my videos." She is focused on choices and variety. Clearly an Options buyer.

▶ ▶ ▶

Remember, buyers are motivated to work in different environments. Some of them like to work in a structured way (like an accountant), while others favor a free-thinking approach (like an artist). Understanding this is the first (and fastest) clue as to whether a person makes decisions through Options or Procedures. To help you sell, you want to know if the person likes to have alternatives available before making a decision or prefers to follow specific, established procedures. Ask the buyer, "Why did you choose to X?" And once you get your response, dig deeper, so you get clarity on exactly how the buyer in front of you approaches decision making.

CHAPTER 6

Big Picture Buyers vs. Detail-Oriented Buyers

SEE THE SQUID? I'm honeymooning with my honey. We're on a sailing ship in the Virgin Islands. We stop in a natural harbor and grab snorkeling gear to explore some incredible underwater wildlife.

We're in about six feet of water and I am stunned by the vision below me. I've never seen anything like it, never heard of it, either—and I grew up in Southern California, hitting the beach at every opportunity.

I pop up and call to Wendy to look down. She looks and sees nothing.

"Look at the seabed, everywhere!" I yell, energy and excitement adding power to my voice.

Head down, head up, head shaking—she doesn't see it.

"Squid!" I tell her. "Baby squid, everywhere!"

Now she sees. The seabed is coated with tens of thousands of baby squid.

Every time we moved, the squid rotated to watch us, little black eyes shifting to monitor our movements. Wild, cool, incredible experience.

Back on the boat, Wendy told me that she didn't see the animals because all she was looking at was a mass of beautiful blue water above and a colorful mass of land below. The details were invisible to her.

In that moment I had an insight into my wife that would give me some distinct information about how she prefers to receive or transmit information.

You may have heard the term *chunking*. A person who chunks *up* is oriented toward the big picture, a global perspective. A person who chunks *down* likes to attend to details.

Do you see how this insight can have an impact on the way you make a sales presentation? Global-oriented buyers want an overview of the impact this decision has on the company. Detail-oriented buyers need to know the steps, the pieces they can count on, in order to take on your solution.

This is one of the easiest traits to identify. It's also one of the easiest to use when you sell. Does the person prefer to look at the big picture or the details? In psychology it's called "scope."

There isn't any special question for learning the secret to how the individual you are speaking with prefers to view the world. I coach sales pros to simply say: "So, as I share information you need to better decide how you'd work with us, would you prefer I give a big picture overview, or do you want all the details?"

Let's say a company vice president wants to buy new hardware for the marketing and advertising division. You ask him flat out for his preference. One buyer might say, "Give me a general description of the cost of the equipment and why this purchase would be good for my department." He's a big picture buyer.

In contrast, another person might answer your question with a litany of requirements, such as, "I need to know which operating system would be included, how much RAM and hard drive space is on each machine, and exactly how your offering would integrate with each of the primary software packages we use to design ads and manage our e-mail campaigns." Specific enough for you? This person is a detail-oriented buyer.

Not surprisingly, to motivate big picture buyers, offer information that will give them a generalized understanding of the issue and don't get involved in detailing every little element related to the decision. To motivate buyers who operate by having every detail at their fingertips, get down into all the pieces of the decision-making puzzle and load them up with information they like to have in hand.

CHAPTER 7

Four Kids in a Classroom

YOU GOTTA BELIEVE ME . . . Scene from the classic film *The Blues Brothers:* John Belushi, as Jake Blues, is kneeling in the mud at the feet of his ex-fiancée (Carrie Fisher). She is pointing an M16 rifle at him. After hunting him down, the jilted woman has decided to kill him, and his brother, Elwood, because Jake left her at the altar.

Jake is about to make the sales pitch of his life. Because if he doesn't convince this woman that she should give him another chance, he loses not an opportunity, but his life.

He clasps his hands together as if praying and fires off his pitch. . . .

Jake: Oh, please don't kill us. Please, please don't kill us. You know I love ya, baby, I wouldn't leave ya. It wasn't my fault.

Fiancée (centering the rifle on his chest): You miserable slug. You think you can talk your way out of this? You betrayed me.

At this point, Jake rattles off every conceivable excuse: He ran out of gas. He had a flat tire. He didn't have enough money for cab fare and his tux did not come back from the cleaners. An out-of-town friend stopped by. Someone stole Jake's car. There was an earthquake. A flood. Locusts.

You can see her eyes melt as she decides to believe that her man was a victim of circumstances. The sale and ensuing kiss are consummated, and Jake makes his getaway.

Impressive pitch. But is there really any way to convince someone of anything?

The answer is *yes*, if you have the wisdom to know how to use the other person's own decision-making process to create conviction. Now, there is no guarantee that this technique works to perfection. You could do everything right and still not land the sale. But you can bet that as you begin to improve your understanding and use of these *Secret Language of Influence* techniques, you'll close more sales than you have in the past.

There are three parts to the convincer strategy:

1. Match your buyers' "dialect."

2. Match their "certainty" pattern.

3. Match their "criteria" for making this decision.

You'll learn here first how to discover each of these three elements, then how to speak directly to the buyer, matching the buyer's way of working through a purchasing decision.

Match Their Dialect

One of the foundational concepts in the application of cognitive psychology to selling is the understanding that people process information in three basic ways.

- *They are visual.* Visual people use expressions like, "Looks good," or "I don't see it," or "That's a great view of the situation." You might say this type of person likes viewing movies.

▸ *They are auditory.* People with an auditory style share who they are by using phrases like, "Sounds good to me," or "That rings a bell," or "We're on the same wavelength." You might say this person likes listening to music.

▸ *They are kinesthetic (i.e., tactile, feeling).* These individuals use words like, "You drove that point home," or "Get a grip," or "That's a solid explanation." You might say these people like engaging their physical self in sports or work or hobbies.

You can find greater detail on these visual, auditory, and kinesthetic (VAK) styles in Chapter 13, on listening skills. Because your ability to pick up these dialects is critical to potent communication skills, that chapter will teach you how to listen and respond properly to the buyer's preferred dialect.

We also want to recognize a fourth way people process information during decisionmaking, which is through reading.

So, the first step in your convincer strategy is to identify whether your buyer prefers information shared visually, auditorily, kinesthetically, or through reading. I like to approach it as if you are working with four kids in a classroom. To identify the buyer's preference, you have to ask "How do you know?" questions.

For instance, "How do you know you chose the right car for you?" Here is how the buyer might answer (note the italicized words that cue this buyer's dialect):

"It's great *looking!*"

"Love the *sound* system!"

"*Handles* like a dream!"

"I *read* a review in *Consumer Reports*, which said this car is a best buy because it has fewer problems and should retain its value."

I strongly suggest you practice asking "How do you know?" questions with people you know, so you can develop some skill at picking up the language. As I suggested at the outset of this book, these practices are totally organic. They can be used in your professional and personal life.

According to research by Rodger Bailey, a therapist and brain/behavior expert who pioneered a great deal of the work on influence, in work settings these dialects break down as follows:

Preferred Dialect	Percentage of People in Workplace
Visual	55
Auditory	30
Kinesthetic	3
Inclined to read	12

Once you have identified your buyers' dialect (with practice, you can identify this preference well before getting into presentation mode for a sales call), you next want to understand how they overcome caution in their personal decision-making process.

Match Their Certainty Pattern

Here's a fact of life in sales: Buyers need to know that they are making the safest decision for their company and for their own job (because careers are made or broken on good or bad decisions).

The certainty pattern is about understanding what it takes for a buyer to feel safe. If you've ever been in the audience for my keynote speech, you may recall that at this teaching moment, I play a song to represent the seller—"Take a Chance on Me," by Abba—and a song to represent the buyer—"Honesty," by Billy Joel.

See, the seller is begging the buyer to say *yes*, hoping for something good to happen. The buyer just wants the truth—honest information—so he can safely make a decision.

I remember meeting a human resources executive who bought (from someone else) a $500,000 program that helped digitize and automate the company's global recruiting efforts. "It didn't really work that well." Those were the actual words he used when he told me that he was now only able to authorize up to $10,000 in expenses before running any buying decision past a board.

The man was fearful of making another bad decision, regardless of the size of the investment. Worse, a poor choice had probably wrecked his career path.

Safety, certainty—how does the buyer know it's the right time to say *yes*? You'll find this issue is fascinating, for yourself, as well as when applied to your profession.

HOW MUCH TIME?

People become convinced over time. The question is, How much time does it take for you to convince someone? Four answers apply here. Your job is to figure out which one applies to the buyer you are sitting across from today.

1. *Some buyers automatically accept information.* That's it. Simply provide information to the prospect and you get instant credibility. Now while it's nice that these people are easily convinced, this means they are easily convinced by everyone—including the competition! It's important that you close this individual quickly before the buyer encounters another option. If you are presenting your solution, along with multiple vendors, you would prefer to be last.

2. *Others are convinced only after a certain number of exposures to your data.* It might take three meetings, three mailings, three phone conversations. You'll need to discover the magic number for each buyer. Once you meet this criterion for certainty, this person becomes a solid, loyal buyer. Why? Because unless another person (i.e., the new seller) recognizes the buyer needs to revisit content multiple times, the person will remain unconvinced.

3. *Others are convinced over a longer period of time.* Three months? Ouch! Can you wait that long? Can your company? People who take a long time to attain certainty are at the root of that evil phrase all sales pros hate: "I'll think it over." These buyers can be maddening. Just be smart enough to ask them how long they need to think it over and you'll be fine, should you choose to wait. My thought here is to move on to other, warmer

prospects and don't worry about these buyers until their time arrives. This doesn't mean you should stay disconnected, but don't put a lot of energy into this prospect.

4. *Others need a consistent diet of information to be convinced.* The secret—and the danger—here is that these buyers are never really convinced. So you can chase them a long, long time without a happy ending. I like to challenge these buyers by asking whether it's unlikely that they'll ever buy my solution. Eventually you might land a sale; enjoy the surprise, but be smart about where you invest your time and energy. All opportunities are not alike.

HOW OFTEN?

Once you understand the buyer's time-based certainty patterns (i.e., can decide immediately, three months from now, or needs a long time), you now have to identify what type of convincing it takes to attain certainty. Be direct. Ask the buyer a simple question, such as:

> How many times do you need to see this type of
> information/research in order to be certain of its value?

Find your own words, your own way to express this question, but make sure you get your buyers to suggest to you what their need is. Don't forget to lay in their dialect when you speak with them. You might say:

> How many times do you think we'd need to get together? (kinesthetic)

> How often should we meet and see (visual) one another?

> How often do you want to have a conversation (auditory) or review (read) the information?

Match Their Criteria for Making This Decision

Our three-part convincer strategy still has another step. To sell people, you need to know *exactly* what they want. You can't guess. You can't hope that your marketing literature or website will show the right bullet points or hit some key chord or grab them with a feeling that matches their need. This may surprise you, but what you have to offer, what you have in your marketing literature, and what you think is true might not be what the buyer has in her head. You have to know exactly what the buyer needs to say *yes*.

Your ability to elicit your buyers' criteria for making their decision is critical throughout the sales process. You can start by using a question you should recognize from Chapter 2, where I talked about To and Away buyers: *What is important to you about X?* (Or, alternatively: *Why is having X important for you?*) Listen carefully as your buyers tell you the specific things they want. Identify whether they are oriented toward attaining benefits (*To* buyers) or solving problems (*Away* buyers).

Now you have a baseline for advancing the conversation based on the buyer's exact wants and needs.

Here's an example. Let's say the buyer is in the market for a new suit. Now listen for his response to the "What's important to you?" question:

> "What's important to me is that the suit is high-quality, so others see me in the best light. And it has to be the perfect color to match my hair and skin tone. I want to look like a spokesperson for a Fortune 100 company."

This person is benefits- and goal-oriented; he told you exactly what he wants. Note, too, that he is visual.

If you don't get enough detail to match your solution to the buyer's criteria, dig deeper by asking a follow-on question like, "Great, tell me more about that." You'll get there. Be patient, and ask smart questions that direct the buyer down a path, which will give you the insights you need to close the sale.

▸ ▸ ▸

The convincer strategy is all about understanding how people filter information in order to gain certainty that something is okay, good, safe. Three elements of this strategy include understanding and mirroring their dialect, discovering how often they need to be certain of this decision, and the specific criteria they have for saying *yes* to you.

KEY TIP: Which kid in the classroom are you? Do you know your dialect? Do you know your certainty pattern? Most people don't know either, though dialect is quite simple to figure out. Make the effort and identify each about yourself. Then you will be able to better recognize these qualities in your buyers. Finally, set down clear criteria for each of your decisions, in order to make better choices in both your personal and professional life.

CHAPTER 8

Critical Language Tips

GOLD COINS—REAL, PURE GOLD . . . The words you use as a sales professional are your gold coins. One of the world's most brilliant word-masters was comedian George Carlin. He juggled words and phrases, directing them to wonderful, unexpected destinations. Ponder this observation:

> *Although the photographer and the art thief were very good friends, neither had ever taken the other's picture.*

So, why include a quote from a comedian in a book on influence? Because comedians, authors, and sales professionals all *make money with their words.*

Therein lies the true power of language: We can manufacture words and phrases and from them produce fruit in the form of revenue.

Sadly, sensitivity to language usage is the most neglected area of sales training (in fact, this is also true of training in leadership, management, and customer service). I am intimately familiar with most major selling systems. They don't (or won't) focus on teaching exact wording for phone or face-to-face selling. This can be disastrous, because it is the little words that can create or kill a sale.

I've read that the average person spends at least one-fifth of her life talking. Ordinarily, in a single day enough words are used to fill a fifty-page book. In one year's time, the average person's words would fill 132 books, each containing 400 pages! Please pay more attention to your word choices. Even a small change can have a large impact on your performance.

The intention in this chapter is to teach you how to be very, very sensitive to words. Your mastery of words will pay you well.

There are seven language strategies that will increase your power to influence prospects. You need to learn how certain word choices can damage opportunity (AVOID) and what to say instead (ADOPT). These critical language tips are categorized as follows:

1. Minimizers

2. "But . . ."

3. "Might"

4. Presuppositions

5. Euphemisms

6. "Why?"

7. Mind-reading

Minimizers

These are words that erode the value of our conversation and therefore our product offering. Examples are the use of words such as *only* or *just*. Placing these words into a sentence undermines the impact of the presentation. In other words, they reduce the value of everything that follows.

AVOID: I grew up being taught to open sales calls with the phrase "I *only* want to talk about . . ." Do you really want to begin a relationship by positioning your ideas as minimal in importance? Do you want to send a message that your product or service is not worth serious and immediate attention? Minimizers do just that. Often, a gatekeeper to the decision maker will unconsciously pick up on those two words—*only* or *just*—and dump you into the "not really important" category. You just helped him keep the buyer from dealing with matters of low-level concern (that would be you). Delete these minimizers from your dialogue when selling on the phone and face-to-face.

ADOPT: Instead, be distinct in your opening statements that your solutions have high value for the buyer. Use comments such as, "This is critical information. Our clients use us to eliminate three key problems that you're probably encountering now." Instead of reducing the value of your offering, you've presented some strong language with a bit of intrigue. (The prospect is now wondering, What are those three issues?)

"But..."

In contrast to minimizers, this one word—in a flash—wrecks everything that comes before it. This is an easy one to recognize, because it can contradict and antagonize.

AVOID: "I want to give you a better price, but . . ." You are saying you don't really want to.

ADOPT: Instead, use the word *and* as a connecter. "I want to give you a better price, and here's what we have to do for that to take effect." This presents a completely different tone. It's a peacemaker and unifies ideas that you state before and after using the word.

There's a nice wordplay you can also use to turn the word *but* to your advantage. You can tell buyers that they can choose the other vendor or solution, "*but* you get what you pay for." This implies someone can make a choice, and it can be a bad one.

"Might"

This is a lame, spineless word. Poor communicators choose limp words. This one is an interesting paradox. Here's a word that, depending on context, can represent strength: "Microsoft is a mighty powerful player in the software market." Yet it is most often used to show weakness.

AVOID: "I *might* be able to adjust the price. . . ." Wow, let's just leave the buyer hanging! We complain that there are no clear next steps and then actually create stalls of our own.

ADOPT: Take a position, be a pro. You can state your position in many ways without wimping out. For example:

"We cannot adjust the price. Our offering is so much better than our competitors'. The trade-off is obvious."

"Price isn't something I can negotiate. I will speak to my senior sales executive and we can sit down again in two or three days. Let's set the talk time right now."

"I would adjust the price when you give us a three-year contract." (Did you catch the *when*, rather than *if*?)

Once you make statements in a selling environment that show you are powerless, it's almost impossible to regain credibility and power. Learn to use strong words—not *might*—when you sell.

Presuppositions

These are words that can unconsciously reference beliefs. *If* and *when* are the most common words we use, often unintentionally. What's the difference between these two phrases?

"If you become a client . . ."

"When you become a client . . ."

There's a world of difference here. Do you hope the buyer will buy (*if*) or believe the buyer will buy (*when*)?

While the buyer might not overtly pick up the difference, her unconscious mind knows that the word *if* reveals that the salesperson sitting across from her is unsure of his offering. The buyer's mind asks, "Why is that?" The buyer is left to wonder if there's something the sales rep isn't sharing. Warning signals begin to ring in her brain. A salesperson lacking confidence has just undermined the sale with a tiny, two-letter presupposition. "When" creates a future. "If " kills it.

The question I ask sales pros in training is whether they plan for the future or let it happen to them.

The only situation where you might use the word *if* to your advantage is to suggest a counterexample or unintended consequence to the buyer's decision. For example, "You can choose that other solution, *if* a lesser result is adequate for you."

Essentially, great sales pros do not use hope, or *if,* as a strategy. They believe it is in the best interest of the buyer to buy their solution. So they say *when.*

Euphemisms

These are safe words that deny reality. They are used to discuss uncomfortable ideas. George Carlin "passed away." "My dog was put down." You don't want to use the difficult words *died* or *killed.* Euphemisms are closely related to ambiguous words that can have multiple meanings. Look at this example from theologian G. K. Chesterton:

> *The word* good *has many meanings. For example, if a man were to shoot his grandmother at a range of 500 yards, I should call him a good shot, but not necessarily a good man.*

As a sales professional, be very wary of undefined or unclear words that muddle the true meaning of a phrase.

My favorite proof of how badly mediocre sales reps handle ambiguous comments comes when they encounter the No. 1 phrase that prospects use to put off sellers. When keynoting, I'll offer this phrase to the sounds of moans and shaking heads (okay, so maybe not all the shaking heads have that rattling sound that comes from having a brain that's a bit smaller than its packaging). Here it is:

We're okay with our current situation.

Upon hearing that phrase, bad reps bail and usually say something feeble like, "Uh, then, can I call you in six months . . . ?"

Great reps don't let buyers deflect or throw them off. They ask for clarity. In that one statement there are three places we can seek clarity: *we, okay,* and *current situation.*

▸ In response to any *"We"* remark, ask: "Who else is involved in this decision?"

▸ Who knows what *okay* means, exactly? If you are feeling brave or have some level of rapport with the buyer, you can try saying something like, "Wow, 'okay' to me sounds mediocre. Are your current solutions great or simply adequate?"

▸ What exactly does *current situation* mean, too? When you want to have fun with these words, try something along the lines of: "You mean everything is going well with the company that sold you your current [product or service]?" Here, we reverse the use of a euphemism by tagging the current vendor as someone who "sold" the buyer. Of course, nobody likes to be *sold*. In this case, we want to be developing a *relationship* to replace the person who *sold* that company. (By the way, this is one of the best ways you can break down objections. For additional applications of this powerful technique, spend some time on Chapter 12, on handling objections.)

By the way, euphemisms infect our sales lives at every level. Some companies choose to keep the term *sales* out of titles, instead using *advisers* or *account executives*. While there is some solid image management being done here (affluent people prefer to deal with advisers), remember that we are who we are—sales professionals. We go to the bank when we sell.

"Why?"

Why is a horrible word and should be abandoned by sales professionals. It serves as an indictment on the intelligence of the person hearing it. The following story, derived from an article I wrote at my website SalesAutopsy.com, depicts a true selling blunder. It shows exactly how damaging one small word can be.

WHY YOU SHOULD NEVER ASK WHY

Jennifer has just spent two hours attempting to sell a software program to a vice president of sales. She has shown every piece of marketing literature she carries. She has answered every question the man asked. It is showdown time.

VP of Sales: Well, I just don't think we are prepared to make a decision today. (The man flashes a courtesy smile and shakes his head.)

Jennifer (referring to an earlier benefit): Why wouldn't you be interested in reducing your sales team's prospecting time by 40 percent?

The smile freezes on the VP's face, and his eyes narrow with Clint Eastwood–like intensity. The man stands, shakes hands, and thanks the sales rep for her visit. Jennifer realizes that she won't be celebrating a big sale over a steak dinner tonight.

What really happened here? Jennifer made a Tyrannosaurus-size mistake. She's angry; stomach acid sizzles inside. After all, hasn't she just invested two hours in educating the prospect about her product? But she forces a smile and responds, according to her training, with a "why" question (hey, it's exactly what I was taught to do in the eighties as well).

Jennifer put the final nail in her commission coffin by choosing one wrong word. When she threw the word *why* into that sentence, she questioned the decision-making ability of that decision maker. *Why* implies that he is stupid.

Think about it. She just gave him thirty-seven great reasons to buy, and he said *no*. The question she really asked him was, "Are you an idiot after hearing all of that? Could you tell me *why* wouldn't you be interested in reducing your sales team's prospecting time by 40 percent?"

Why has a dark history; its roots lie in poor parenting techniques. So you can assume almost everyone has encountered a situation similar to this one:

You're sixteen years old and have just announced to your parents that you're going to hitchhike to Mexico and try cliff diving with some friends. Dad looks at you and says, "*Why* in the world would you do that? *Why* would anyone throw a perfectly good body 100 feet into an ocean? That's unbelievably dumb, what a stupid decision. Did I raise an idiot? Blah, blah, blah. Why, why, why?"

Do you recall having a parent or other adult talk to you like that? Do you think it's a smart move to throw the prospect's unconscious mind back to that time when he was verbally beaten up for a choice he made?

Is it wise to imply that your solution is so good, so obvious, that only a fool would pass it up?

Good news! You can replace *why* with another word that gives you loads of information and will help you keep the call from ending prematurely. Your new word is *how*.

Whereas "why" creates a defensive response, "how" respectfully asks about the buyer's decision-making process. Let's put our new word to work on Jennifer's sales VP buyer.

VP of Sales *(flashing a stiff smile and shaking his head):* Well, I just don't think we are prepared to make a decision today.

Jennifer: Oh. *How* did you determine that we're not right, at this time, for you?

Using *how* discards the "in your face" indictment of the prospect's intelligence. It turns the question into a request for understanding the *process* that a buyer has gone through to reach his decision. Understanding this concept is worth the weight of this book in gold. Notice also that Jennifer sneaked in the phrase "at this time," to imply that momentarily she's all right with the buyer's resistance. But it is the way she asks the how question that offers the real power in this dialogue. Pay close attention to the psychology at work here. You want to draw out of your buyers the process or path they travel to get to a decision. Asking how will help you unpack the buyer's brain and discover how that individual makes up his mind.

> *KEY TIP: Ask the "how" question at the start of the sales call. For instance, "How did you decide we should be sitting down to talk today?" You'll learn your buyer's thought process right up front. The buyer might say, "I read your literature, then ran it by some of my team, who said, 'Yes, it's a good idea to bring Dan in to discuss redesigning our existing sales training program.'" In this instance, I've just discovered the buyer is influenced by reading material and by external input from others. (Revisit Chapter 4 for profiles of internal vs. external buyers.)*

One word of caution, though: Most prospects will hear you asking *why* even when you deliberately use the term *how*. They will give the quick answer and not describe the process you want to hear. You'll have to ask the question again, gently, perhaps worded differently, but once again emphasizing the how. You may need to tell the prospect that you are asking about the process he engages in to decide whether to take on a new product or service. I'll gesture with my hands sometimes, moving them from right to left, or left to right, stopping a few times as if to show the steps along a path. The unspoken message to the buyer is that I'm wondering how his mind works its way along the path of reasoning.

Take this wisdom and walk away with it. Replace the word *why* with *how*. Do it today, and do it in your vocabulary at work and home. Isn't it a big personal bonus to understand how your family and friends make decisions? Pay close attention to the words you use and the words you feed to others. Your elevated communication skills will make you more money at work and draw you closer to people you care about.

Mind-Reading

We may think we understand someone's beliefs, but then we stumble when we don't ask for a clear picture or verbal clarification of the other person's position. An old Henny Youngman joke teaches this concept as well.

One time I came home and my wife was crying. I asked her what happened. She said, "I knew you'd have a hard day of work, so I baked your favorite, a cherry pie. But the dog ate it."

"Don't cry," I told her, "I'll buy you another dog."

He misread her mind, believing she was upset because the food killed the dog, not because of her hard work baking the now-lost cherry pie.

Mind-reading is actually the basis for most situation comedy shows on television. One person makes a statement that is misinterpreted by another character. And off they go with two different beliefs that collide, confusing everyone until the misunderstanding is cleared up. In the meantime, laughs abound.

MIND-READING MISFORTUNE

Unfortunately, it's not much of a joke when sales professionals ignore the hidden meaning behind a question or comment. In another Sales Autopsy.com fan favorite (and there are plenty, as I've collected over 600 sales horror stories), this blunder costs a rep, named Tim, a sale while providing a lesson for everyone else.

Here, in Tim's own words, is the story of how he made a wrong guess and ended up losing eighty-five customers:

Cecil was ancient and about to retire. As president of his company, he was determined to see that his insurance needs were cared for—as well as those of his eighty-four employees.

As a sales manager I was working with a new sales rep on this "orphan" account. Our company specializes in insurance benefits through payroll deduction. No one had enrolled in any new insurance programs in this group in over five years.

My new agent and I could hardly believe it! We were just days away from significant commission checks. As the new agent and I were opening our calendars to schedule a group seminar for the eighty-five employees, Cecil asked us if we offered long-term care (LTC) insurance. Pumped with excitement and thinking I could perhaps even write his personal LTC policy that day, I said, "Of course we do. In fact, I believe we have one of the best in the industry. I also believe that everyone over age 50 should seriously consider purchasing LTC."

I will never forget the look on Cecil's face. It was as if I told him that his grandchildren were fat and ugly. After what felt like three hours of silence, Cecil told me that he had looked at LTC literature from several companies and had come to the conclusion that this type of insurance was "a bunch of crap." Furthermore, he told me that if I thought LTC was a good idea I obviously didn't know my head from a hole in the ground and there was no way he was going to do business with me. The intensity of his language and the expression on his face made it clear—there was no way to recover from my mistake.

Needless to say, we went from closing the deal to getting shut out of the company. I learned not to mind-read when responding to something someone says.

Tim accurately analyzed his mistake. He should have responded to the buyer's question about LTC insurance with another question. A safe one would have been simply, "Please tell me what information you are seeking," or "What are you trying to figure out about LTC?" Either would have been a smarter response.

On the other hand, I did once have someone teach me how to use mind-reading to my advantage. Tony Jeary is a great friend and is recognized as "Coach to the World's Top CEOs" (www.tonyjeary.com). A few years ago I spent a day with him in Texas, reviewing my keynote content and videotaping my presentation. He suggested I do a *mind-read* to open my next speaking program.

Two weeks later I was back in Dallas, standing in front of 600 sales pros at a global sales conference. After I was introduced my first words were, "Okay, be honest. How many of you wonder if I have anything good to say? You've read all the sales books, listened to tapes and CDs, heard all the speakers. How many of you are wondering if this guy has anything unique or useful or even interesting to say?" I raised my hand to encourage their response, and hundreds of arms crept up as the audience members admitted their skepticism.

I went right into my opening tale, a hilarious horror story where a sales rep thinks a picture of a prospect and his wife is really the prospect and football broadcaster John Madden. The punch line was met with twenty-six seconds of laughter. I was shocked (a comedian would kill for just fifteen seconds).

But the contrast between my mind-read (i.e., the audience is expecting nothing new) and my story of a very funny, embarrassing blunder actually elevated the level of delight and surprise. The CEO in charge of this sales conference grabbed me when I got offstage and said to me, "Dan, you nailed us with your opening line. We were all skeptical until you started to teach us some great strategies using your funny stories."

In this instance, my coach's advice to use mind-reading created a special moment that endeared me to my client and his sales team. (I've since done quite a bit of business with the company.) Just be careful, though: If mis-handled, mind-reading—like euphemisms and ambiguous words—can produce bad results in sales and actually obscure your understanding of what the buyer is really thinking. Always use direct questions to discover the buyer's "truth."

▸ ▸ ▸

In summary, these seven language elements must be tightly controlled by the strongest muscle in our bodies—our tongue. An old proverb says that the tongue is like a small bit that turns a large horse, a small rudder that steers a large ship (even when great winds are present), and a tiny spark that sets a large forest on fire. The tongue is strong enough to both build up and tear down.

How will you choose to use your newly uncovered speaking skills? I trust that your awareness of the power of language will help you build up both your sales career and your bank account.

Become a master of using words wisely. This should be your strongest desire in attaining world-class selling skills.

CHAPTER 9

Evoke Emotions!

AAAAAHHHHH! (AND OTHER EXPRESSIONS THAT HELP YOU SELL) . . . I've always wanted to use that as a chapter title in a book. I love the sound of it. And honestly, I struggled between using *Aaaarrrggghhh!* and *Aaaaahhhhh!* I believe you'll agree that I chose the right one.

The point of that expression? It represents an emotion, an outburst of feeling. *Say it again, right now.* Did it come flying off your tongue as a good feeling, or one of disgust, possibly despair?

Understanding emotions is one of the least understood, and certainly least taught, concepts in selling. Here's the teaching that I want you to walk away with:

You must evoke emotion when you converse with prospects.

How best to do this? By crafting your questions so that they create not simply a logical but a gut response from your buyers.

How do we know that emotiveness is important? How do we know it works? Neuroeconomics tells us it does. The study of neuroeconomics is a combination of research from the fields of psychology, economics, and neuroscience. It looks at the role of the brain when we evaluate decisions, categorize risks and rewards, and interact with one another. And almost every study on decision making reveals that when buyers decide to buy, they are driven by emotion first, then validate or rationalize with logic.

Now that last statement is no news to sales pros. We've been aware of the truth of it for years. But we've never been trained to create an emotional context to our conversations.

When you come to believe that evoking emotion during a sales call is key to helping buyers decide to buy, you will intentionally develop questions and comments that help your prospects get caught up in the emotion of the moment. It's not that you are fooling someone into feeling something. Rather, you are drawing out context that most buyers suppress during a sales call.

If you neglect to create an environment where an emotional response occurs, you'll end up with a clinical, rational prospect who decides with his head, not his heart. If this idea fascinates you and you want more information, you'll be captivated by the stories, research, and applications from Jonah Lehrer's book, *How We Decide.*

The corporate marketing world understands this notion quite well. I know it's scary to admit marketing could teach sales something, since our egos normally believe it works in reverse. But take this lesson to heart (where emotion rules the day, anyway). As an example, BMW created an automobile commercial that illustrates this point:

> *What you make people feel is as important as what you make.*
> *We don't just make cars, we make joy!*

The commercial is accompanied by many images, all connected with the word *joy,* a powerful emotion.

It's time for sales pros in America to intentionally adopt these practices as well.

All of the questioning strategies detailed in this book center on evoking emotion first. That means we need to understand the emotional component of every benefit we offer and every problem solved by our products and/or services.

When prospects make decisions, either they will choose based on benefits or good things they get, or they will be motivated to take action and buy in order to avoid some problem in the present or the future. We covered this concept in Chapter 2. Your job is to develop questions that generate either positive or negative emotions, and to match the proper emotion to the buyer's style, be it benefits-based or problem-oriented. Here are a few examples of these emotional responses. (For a more comprehensive list, see the EARL chart of forty-eight emotions near the end of the chapter.)

Positive Emotions	Negative Emotions
Excitement	Disgust
Empathy	Irritation
Hope	Fear
Calm	Embarrassment
Surprise	Stress

You reinforce the power of emotion when you ask your questions by directly inserting a bit of feeling. Let's say, for example, that a buyer tells you about a certain bad experience. You respond by saying: "You had customized books ordered for your national sales conference and they arrived at the end of the event? Oh no! What did your boss say?"

Now you might assume that the "Oh no!" shows you are empathetic to the bad experience (akin to Bill Clinton's classic "I feel your pain"), but the boss question is a really rough one. Your buyer will most likely go right back to that place and time where his manager, executive, or owner teed off on the poor person for letting this mistake happen in the first place.

Your follow-up comment might be, "We will never let anything like that happen to you again." That comment gets emotions back on track for the buyer, as he will begin to experience hope, satisfaction, trust, or relief (all identified in our list of emotions).

Once again, your job is to evoke emotion and form a bond with the buyer throughout the sales process. There are literally dozens of questions for each step in the selling process. Remember the reference I made to a recently designed sales training program for one financial services firm where we crafted thirty-seven questions to use with prospects, including this crazy response?

Prospect: We're too old to buy an annuity.

Salesperson: Not really, we have sea turtles older than you as clients.

Laughter (and surprise) generates a gut response that spikes emotion and bonds you with your buyer. By the way, this response can be safely said to a buyer only when you have a big smile on your face that exhibits joy, friendliness, or delight—great emotions. If you didn't smile the comment could come off sarcastically, showing disgust or annoyance, two negative emotions.

Here are sample questions, categorized according to the stage in the selling process where they can be used. If you don't find your voice among the following five responses to some of the basic pieces of the selling puzzle, create your own—and add emotion to increase their potency in front of those prospects. In these examples, the words that inject emotion into the question are italicized. Don't forget that your facial expressions, tone, and even gestures must support the emotion you are emphasizing and reinforce your empathy with the buyer's current condition.

Qualifying and Disqualifying
How fast do we want to get this *frustrating* selection made and off your plate, so you can get back to your other responsibilities?

Clarifying the Buying and Decision-Making Process
Do you *battle* a board that helps make this decision, or will they pretty much rubber-stamp anything you like?

Defining Success, Goals, and Problems That Need Attention
You've had some *stressful* vendor relationships in the past. What's the best way to let you know you've made the right choice here?

Finalizing the Sale

So, when I give you a proposal with the numbers we discussed and the timing that fits, you'll be *happy* to get started, won't you?

Following Up with the New Client

Is everything good? You *happy*? Can I do anything differently to make things *easier* for you?

I coach sales pros to act as if they were talking to a best friend, to the point where they could grab the buyer by the shoulders, shake him, and say, "You've got to have this! Your life will be changed forever with a simple *yes!*" You get the picture—your own emotions reveal the depth of your belief in your solutions.

Before you go put everything I've advised into play, let's once more quickly review two essential points:

1. *Don't underestimate the emotional component of questioning.* Remember the research data on how decisions are made—they are first based on emotions. You must build emotional word choices into your questions.

2. *Find your voice.* That is, make sure the questions you use reflect your personality and your actual vocabulary. Make sure you ask questions with authentic interest in the answers, and use emotion in your voice and face as well.

Let's look at a list of emotions, to give you a better idea of how to evoke them during your sales dialogues.

EMOTIONS BY THE DOZENS

The HUMAINE Association, a professional, worldwide network of researchers in the field of emotion-oriented/affective computing, has developed the Emotion Annotation and Representation Language (EARL) that classifies forty-eight emotions. Here is your chart of these forty-eight emotions.

EARL chart of emotions.

Negative Thoughts	Positive Thoughts
Doubt	Courage
Envy	Hope
Frustration	Pride
Guilt	Satisfaction
Shame	Trust
Negative and Forceful	**Positive and Lively**
Anger	Amusement
Annoyance	Delight
Contempt	Elation
Disgust	Excitement
Irritation	Happiness
	Joy
	Pleasure
Negative and Passive	**Quiet Positive**
Boredom	Calm
Despair	Content
Disappointment	Relaxed
Hurt	Relieved
Sadness	Serene
Negative and **Not in Control**	**Reactive**
Anxiety	Interest
Embarrassment	Politeness
Fear	Surprise
Helplessness	
Powerlessness	
Worry	
Agitation	**Caring**
Shock	Affection
Stress	Empathy
Tension	Friendliness
	Love

Source: HUMAINE Association.

You'll find more on this fascinating topic of emotional connections in Chapter 10, where I discuss the persuasive power of storytelling and share a great story that landed a major sale. I would also love to hear about your experiences focusing on emotional context during selling. Please contact me directly with your stories by e-mail: Dan@GotInfluenceInc.com.

CHAPTER 10

The Persuasive Power of Storytelling in Selling

THE BATTLE OF PLAYLAND (OR A "TALE OF TWO KIDDIES") . . . . I've collected more than 600 hilarious sales stories about blunders committed by our peers. The sheer volume alone of my work writing magazine columns, publishing books, keynoting, and training has forced me to attain a level of expertise in storytelling. Even though I have boatloads of business tales, I'll start this chapter with a personal story.

Rebekah (or Bekah, as she's nicknamed) is four years old, and she's a really good kid. Never does anything wrong, a precious write-off . . . I mean, treasure. And I'm not just saying that because she's my kid. She's never been arrested or anything. Her twin, Abbie, is equally angelic.

One of the reasons our kids are pretty good is that we have a family mission statement:

Be a Blessing

That's it, three words—specific enough and vague enough that each individual can interpret the statement and act on it based on how she is playing with anyone at any given moment. The girls are sent off to school with these words to encourage them to think about building relationships and building up others, rather than being selfish and disrespectful.

Perhaps another reason they've turned out well is that the wife and I did not take Grandma's advice: "You should beat your children every day. If you don't know what *they* did, they do!"

Anyway, I have Abbie and Bekah at a McDonald's Playland. They are excited that they will discover new friends. Often they even remember to ask their names.

An hour into playing, another girl—a big girl, quite a tomboy—cruises to the bottom of the big slide and just sits there. Bekah comes flying down moments later and crashes into her. The girl leaps up, spins around, and glares at my daughter, who stands, staring up at the older girl.

I'm intrigued to see how this situation will be resolved. They face each other, saying nothing.

The girl suddenly spits in Bekah's face.

She turns from Bekah and runs to her parents, who are sitting at a table next to me. They have also watched the collision and standoff. Horrified, they start gathering up their things, telling the girl that they're leaving. No apology, no comment to their kid on her behavior, nothing.

Bekah does nothing as well.

This is interesting. Instead of intervening—calling out to see how my kid feels about what's just happened—I decide to continue watching.

The highly dysfunctional family (I say *highly* because they've just proved they rate well above mine on the dysfunction scale) leaves without a word to me. They walk around the corner of the play area, daughter trailing Mom and Dad.

As the parents disappear, Bekah springs forward toward her enemy, shoving her into the mesh wall of the play area, raising her fists and pounding the bigger girl on the back. I'm shocked! Even as I'm writing this story, I can still hear in my mind the hollow thudding sound of my daughter's fists pounding on that girl.

Abbie, the twin, who has been a silent observer during the incident, runs over and joins her sister. Four little fists are hammering on one back.

I'm stunned at my girls' behavior. But I've got to admit that I did start to laugh. About seventeen blows later, the bigger girl squirms away and bolts for her parents. She never cried out, never retaliated. It was as if she knew she deserved some retribution.

My daughters turn to me with huge smiles on their faces, and I'm gnawing the inside of my cheeks to keep from responding in kind.

I share this story when training sales professionals on the art of storytelling. And I've got to tell you that when I speak the line "The girl suddenly spits in Bekah's face," my audience members very verbally, and visually, react. This is where emotional context really comes into play. Sure, some people have kids and get good feelings thinking about two girls playing together. But that moment both changes and deepens the emotional connection to the story.

When I'm done talking about the experience, I'll mention that my wife, Wendy, was not happy about Bekah's behavior when she later heard about what occurred. Okay, she was more horrified than "not happy."

So what does that story prove? What's the point of it all?

I've been able to use "the incident" to train salespeople on dealing with To and Away buyers (as covered in Chapter 2). In this chapter, you'll learn how a story works on the brain at both a conscious and subconscious level. You'll read about how to use a story on a sales call, with the example of a great story I used to close a very large sale. Finally, you'll find here a model for creating your own personal, emotional, and teachable (PET) stories to use when you sell.

The Battle of the Playland (as Bekah's tale is now known) made me think about one of the great philosophical arguments of all time and how it pertains to us as sales professionals: *Are people inherently good or evil?*

Do we assume that prospects and existing customers are good at heart? Or shall we act on the fact that they all have shades of the dark side living within? The assumption we choose to pursue has an impact on how we physically deal with these characters, as well as how we mentally and emotionally handle them.

And what about the implications for ourselves? Is this topic too deep for the average salesperson? Is this thinking worth putting energy into?

The question you always want to ask when learning is, "Is it useful?"

If it's useful, has value, makes me money, or keeps me from leaving money on the table, I'll address it. Let's look at both sides of the good/evil coin.

If People Are Inherently Good, They Are Probably:

- *Honest.* They tell you the truth because it's the right thing to do. They might withhold information that gives a rep an advantage in bidding or pricing product, but basically they are straightforward in their interactions.

- *Respectful.* They realize you have a job to do, just like them, and they expect other people to want to do their best while winning the game. So they bring a win/win attitude to the table. They return phone calls, even if it's to share bad news.

- *Ethical.* They do the right thing, even if they don't gain from it personally. They don't bludgeon others with their status or position in order to gain an advantage. An ethical mindset is the basis of a person with great character. You know this is someone you'd want your kids to hang out with.

If People Are Inherently Evil, They Are Probably:

- *Selfish.* They want the best for the least. They don't care about your life's work, about whether you get commissions or are profitable. It's all about them, first and last.

- *Rule Benders.* They don't play the buyer/seller game fairly. They may even expect special treatment or favors in order to grant you the business. They simply don't respect rules that exist to keep all players in a business environment honest.

- *Deceitful.* They hide behind voice mail or gatekeepers. They won't tell you what's really going on: who the real decision makers are, how soon they will make a decision, or what other companies they are speaking with. They are untrustworthy and so they don't trust others, thinking that any information shared would hurt their advantage over the salesperson.

So what do you think about your prospects? Are some good, some evil? Or does what *you decide to believe* about them matter more than the truth about the individual?

Your healthiest perspective is to walk into relationships thinking the best of the other person. Speak to people as if they embody goodness and life. Listen to them as if they are as honest and candid as your best friend. Until a specific prospect proves otherwise, take the position that each individual is as good as gold—since, in fact, these individuals do provide cash flow for your family.

As soon as your prospects show their true colors, and those colors are simply shades of black, turn and run. Disqualify them quickly, which is what top salespeople do, and choose to work with people who are so good you'd want them to influence your kids (or borrow my kids, if you have none of your own).

Are buyers inherently good or evil? What they actually are depends on you.

At this point I might wrap up the lesson by encouraging people (this would mean you, now) not to believe anything bad of anyone without seeing firsthand evidence, personal proof. Take the high road when encountering prospects; show respect, energy, and make your best sales effort until they disqualify themselves from consideration.

Here's a fascinating thing about stories. They can have many meanings. In one setting I shared the Battle of the Playland and asked a room of sales reps to decide, at their tables, what the lesson of the story was. Answers were wildly varied. Themes included justice, revenge, coaching, discipline, communication, maturity, decision making, patience, teamwork, modeling, parenting, intervention, and conflict resolution.

This is important to understand because listeners may interpret the value of a story based on their own experience. In fact, in counseling, when hypnosis is used, the counselor knows that the unconscious mind will take what it needs most in that moment and give interpretation to the story.

I once tried to prove this last point at a sales conference when I announced that I was going to hypnotize all 600 attendees. I asked everyone to relax, close their eyes, and listen to a story. Here is what I said:

> You're getting on a plane for an incredible vacation to Australia. There are 365 seats and you're sitting comfortably in one with plenty of legroom. You look around the plane and spot one empty seat. Otherwise, all around you are happy, talkative, soon-to-be tanned tourists. The plane lands and all the travelers are excited about their dream trips. They get to personally see, hear, and experience all the amazing things that embody Australia. There are kangaroos, great white sharks, surfing, scuba diving, wine tours, incredible seafood, and generous friendly people. What fun! This vacation has been amazing.
>
> Thank you, you can open your eyes now. Wasn't that great? Relaxing? Now, who can tell me what that story is really about?

One sales pro leaped out of his seat and shouted his insight. "It's not about the trip, it's about the airplane! There are 365 seats with one empty. That means if we waste one day of our year, we lose opportunities that can never be recovered!"

Game, set, and match. The guy got it. The story, at some level, became a metaphor for life itself.

Just as that airline will never recover the lost revenue from that empty seat—it's gone forever—you would be judicious to increase your awareness of the value of time and using it well. Do you use your days wisely? How about the pieces—the hours and minutes that comprise those days? Every time you waste any time you trash potential income from selling. It is lost forever.

The power of storytelling should be embraced by everyone who sells. I am always sharing stories when I sell. It's captivating and interesting to prospects. Because a story has basic elements that include a beginning, some conflict or highlight, and an ending, listeners wait patiently for it to unfold.

Using Stories in a Sales Setting

My personal favorite is the following narrative, which landed my company a major contract to redesign the client's sales training program.

I'm sitting with the head of global sales training for a major organization you would immediately recognize. A couple of his senior training executives heard me speak on some of the latest ideas (including influence) that companies need to consider adding to their sales training program, so they decided to invite me to company headquarters, where I spend four hours with these key people, discussing my approach to selling.

One of the company's products is an energy drink. I tell the senior executive that I'm curious about how they teach their people, all independent reps, to sell it. He explains: "Let's say some parents are sitting watching a soccer game. Our adviser pops one open and begins to drink it. Another adult says, 'Hey, what is that? It's not Gatorade or Red Bull.' Our independent rep says, 'It's a new energy drink that I sell. I have some in the trunk of my car, if you'd like to buy it and try it.'"

I grimace at the story, and a little "Ooooh" squeezes between my lips.

The VP's eyes go wide and he sits up and says, "What? How would you do it? What would you teach our people to do?"

"Wow," I reply. "You kind of *go for the throat.* I would handle it differently. Take the long way around to the sale."

"How?"

I give him my advice: "When the person asks about the drink, I'd say something like, 'Let me ask you something—are you a morning or afternoon person? Do you have more energy early or later in the day?' When they reply I'd say, 'Really? Tell me more about that.' What you've done is create an emotional connection with the person as well as the product. This is very powerful, and it can significantly increase your people's ability to sell."

The VP stares at me for a few moments, then says, "Dan, I think our sales training really sucks. Would you help redesign it?"

Our first project was an overhaul of a video training program for Latin America. Bigger things are on the horizon.

Specific Ways to Develop Your Own Storytelling When Selling

I use a simple model that employs the elements in the acronym PET:

P Personal

E Emotional

T Teachable (or Trainable)

This PET model is very easy to adapt. Let's cover each element.

MAKE IT PERSONAL

Everyone has personal stories. In a pure business-to-business context, you should be intimately familiar with any evidence or testimonials. By putting your individual spin on these stories of proof, you can better create a telling that captivates your buyer.

For personal tales, you may need to trigger memories to recover them. Mine your memory for:

- *First experiences,* with food, kissing, school, friends, drinks, jobs, speeches, paychecks, and so on. You get the idea. The first time something happens, most people can be nervous, and yet it works out great in the end.

- *Bad blunders,* with awkward comments, accidents, those times when you didn't fit in with a group, got arrested, and so on. Now, create a context that relates to a buyer-seller relationship; for example: "If I were you, Mr./Ms. Buyer, I wouldn't want to have anything like this happen. I'm here to help ensure that it doesn't."

Now you have your content. Let's make sure it really has an impact on your prospect.

BE EMOTIONAL

Your ability to add emotional context to your story is key to having it strike a chord with and move the buyer. Revisit Chapter 9 and the EARL chart of forty-eight types of emotions you can evoke in the telling of your tale.

BE SURE IT'S TEACHABLE

What's the point? Make sure you explain exactly what you want the buyer to take away from the story. Offer your teaching moment with a big smile on your face if you are evoking a positive feeling. But if you are evoking negative emotions, a sympathetic smile and nod can let your buyers know that you are part of the team, on their side, and want to help avoid the problem your story describes.

Pick your PET story, and then craft it to do any of the following things:

- Share success stories that serve as evidence that others were smart enough to buy from you.

- Share warning stories that caution your buyers about the direction they're headed, the cliff at the end of the road, the disaster you can help them avoid.

- Share stories about how heroes are made inside organizations like theirs when they say *yes* to your solutions.

- Share stories that embody the emotions involved in this decision, whether they are positive or negative.

▸ ▸ ▸

Use stories, craft them well, and practice telling them. They can be business tales or personal experiences. But get started today looking for and recording stories to use. Great salespeople can literally hypnotize buyers with stories that have happy endings and that have *you* as the reason everyone wins.

CHAPTER 11

Questions That Advance the Sale Closer to the Close

TRICK QUESTION . . . What is your purpose in asking questions? I'll give you a hint: In Christianity, Judaism, and Islam, there is a story about Moses and the burning bush.

Moses thinks it's amazing. He is gazing at a bush that is burning but is not burning up. Flames are roaring away and the plant remains as green as a golf course. It must be a miracle, and sure enough, God starts speaking. He tosses a question at Moses: "What is that in your hand?"

Now, as the story goes, Moses thinks he has his shepherd's staff in his hand and even answers the question that way—until God tells him to throw it on the ground and the staff turns into a snake. It's a very exciting scene; you can look up the details for yourself.

But your job right now is to answer a question: What is your purpose in asking questions? There's a hint in the story, hidden in God's question: *What is that in your hand?*

Assuming that God is an all-knowing, all-powerful being, there's probably a very good chance that He knows what that stick is. He doesn't need Moses's help here. So why ask?

God is about to challenge Moses's thinking. This is really an interview question to discover if this prospective leader of two million people is a good fit. God asks a question so that the conversation moves in a direction that He wants it to go. That sounds to me like great selling. In other words:

The question is for the benefit of the person being asked.

Wise sales professionals know that great questions are meant to gather information that points to problems they can solve or benefits they offer. Therefore, develop your questions so that they put your prospects on a path of *your* choosing.

Let's practice this concept. Suppose you are selling a car to a woman in sales.

You: Your car's all right. What made you decide to start looking at new ones?

Prospect: Just wanted to upgrade my image a bit.

You: Oh, really? What is that about?

Prospect: I just got a promotion and wanted to make sure what I drive is a reflection of my success.

You: So, what would happen if you kept driving this one?

Prospect: People would probably wonder about my earnings, or I'd be embarrassed to take clients out in this older car.

You: Do clients' attitudes about you affect your business?

Prospect: Yes, in the sense that they like to work with successful people, right? Doesn't everybody?

You get the idea. Your questions are leading her deeper into despair about the impact of not owning a new car. You could continue, following up on her remark about how the car she drives affects her earnings, or asking questions about other problems related to getting out of the old car and into a new one. Your questions could lead another prospect down a different path filled with the benefits of owning a new car—for instance, it has more prestige, it's fun to drive, a fast ride, and "You look great in it," and so on.

Learn to develop great lines of inquiry, and remember this concept: The question is for the benefit of the person being asked.

Great sales professionals ask extraordinary questions. In this chapter you'll gain a rock-solid foundation for your questioning strategy. The learning is structured in three sections:

1. Reasons for Questions

2. Rules for Questions

3. Categories of Questions

Keep one thing in mind as you absorb this information and develop your own list of questions. You must find your "voice." In other words, you have to discover words and phrases that reflect your personality, because then your conversations should attain a comfort level that is close to a simple chat between friends. That way you'll quickly know whether this prospect is worth pursuing or whether it's time to walk away. Remember, in sales you are always qualifying or disqualifying prospects. Your ability to spend time in dialogues with great prospects will enhance your ability to increase sales.

Reasons for Questions: Fifteen Results You Get from Great Questions

1. Rapport is generated and continues to build.

2. The prospect's needs, wants, objectives, goals, and problems are better understood.

3. You'll see how your solutions fit (or don't fit) those concerns.

4. Improved data helps quantify or dollarize the value of your solutions.

5. You get to craft effective responses to objections.

6. The dialogue has direction; take it down a path of your choosing, in order to help the buyer see things he might not be aware of (remember Moses' staff?).

7. You get assurance that the buyer feels safe in her decision making, by addressing worries about how she is perceived in the organization as a decision maker, or how this choice will help the organization save money or attain more of it. Help the buyer realize that she has made the best possible choice among the options (including, of course, your competition).

8. The creation of candor helps the buyer feel comfortable with you personally. Buyers will open up and honestly share information only when they truly believe your interests are in serving them, not simply closing a sale.

9. You have the ability to upsell and cross-sell. Discover all the issues at stake and you realize other ways your solutions could serve the buyer's firm.

10. Emotion is evoked through that casual conversation, which helps to motivate the prospect to take action. This approach is aided, tremendously, by having an air of curiosity about you (a technique covered in greater detail in Chapter 13, on listening).

11. Information is gained through listening first and talking last.

12. Solutions are presented on time, not prematurely (another by-product of good listening).

13. True buyers (or all the buyers) are identified.

14. All the information is nailed down to close the sale.

15. You'll know when it's time to walk away.

Rules for Questions: Five Rules That Lead You to Great Questioning Practices

RULE 1: EVOKE EMOTION WITH YOUR QUESTIONS

It bears repeating: You *must* evoke emotion when you converse with prospects. Your questions have to get buyers to respond with feelings, not just logic. Once they are caught up in the emotion of the moment, whether positive or negative, they will be open to solving the problem (after negative emotions are revealed) or attaining goals (after positive emotions are in play).

Revisit Chapter 9 to develop expertise in designing dialogues that evoke emotions.

Let's look next at another psychologically sound way to use a different form of emotional connectors with buyers.

RULE 2: LEAD WITH SOFTENING STATEMENTS

People's views—and buying decisions—are influenced by their personal background, experience, education, and professional roles. *Softening statements* are a great way not only to acknowledge other people's experience, but also to show respect and empathy for them as business professionals.

Good psychology teaches us that it helps to gain an emotional connection with a prospect by prefacing questions with brief softening statements such as:

"Oh, I just thought of this. . . ."

"Help me out here, please. . . ."

"I appreciate you being honest with me. . . ."

"Oh no!"

"My goodness. . . ."

"I'm curious. . . ."

"I'm not sure exactly what you mean by that. Can you please explain?"

These statements create a conversation that sounds more spontaneous and more like two friends or business colleagues working through the decision together. This approach also prevents *us vs. them* dialogues from occurring, which happens too often in sales.

And we've all been there, we've all experienced what it's like when a sales rep becomes defensive. Here's how it usually plays out: The prospect says, "Your price is too high." And the seller counters, "Not really, when you calculate . . ." Or else the seller says, "By how much?" *or* "We have plenty of clients who decided to buy from us."

Here is the same dialogue with the sales rep using a softening statement. (Take note of how this conversation makes you feel.)

Prospect: Your price is too high.

Seller: Help me out here, please. You're saying it's too high, but is it too high compared to other options, or do you mean you may not have the budget for this amount?

Or . . .

Seller: I just thought of something; let's work through some numbers so that we know for sure what the best decision is for you.

Or . . .

Seller: Oh no! I guess we're done talking then, right?

Never underestimate the power of empathy during sales conversations. Now, let's move on to deepening a prospect's emotional responses.

RULE 3: DIG DEEPER

Here's something good to know. The best questions give you an opportunity not only to evoke a deeper emotional response, but also to understand more details about the prospect's situation. Here are a few examples of areas where you can devise questions that dig deeper:

▸ A loss of income, time, opportunity, promotion, status, business, or job

▶ Poor individual or company performance

▶ Wasted time, money, or energy

When a prospect mentions topics such as these, you would then follow up with comments such as "Tell me more" or "Interesting. What else can you share about that?" or "How has that affected others [the firm, your customers, etc.]?"

By digging deeper you can take the conversation down a path of your choosing. In the questions that follow, notice how the same cost issue can be followed up by another question that then leads the conversation down a different path:

▶ I see . . . so you figured out exactly how much this issue is costing the company. How much longer can you tolerate a relatively slow decision-making process?

—*Path:* buying process, timing

▶ I see . . . so you figured out exactly how much this issue is costing the company. Is it getting so expensive that you might prefer a faster solution vs. a less expensive one?

—*Path:* lost income, value

▶ I see . . . so you figured out exactly how much this issue is costing the company. Who's going to start holding your feet to the fire to resolve this?

—*Path:* decision maker, economic stakeholder

As you identify which path you'll follow, be prepared to ask additional questions to gain clarity on the topic. For example, in the last scenario, follow-up questions could be:

"So, how do you equate that figure's impact on the firm?"

"Is it equal to losing a new sales hire each year, or losing a point of market share?"

You want to make sure that your prospect has a clear picture of the dramatic impact your solution can provide.

RULE 4: IDENTIFY THE TYPES OF AND TIMES FOR QUESTIONS

In this section, we are going to identify what kinds of questions (types) to ask during the different phases (times) of the sale. We'll move chronologically through the sales process, focusing on three main steps. Additional details on other parts of the sales process follow in the Categories of Questions section.

The first step is to qualify or disqualify your prospect. Embedded in this step is your need to uncover whether the person in front of you has budget, urgency, and authority to say *yes*. Each element has three questions.

Budget

We respect your time in working on a solution. Are there financial parameters within which we should be working?

What is your expectation of the investment required?

Would you be willing to share what you're willing to spend?

Urgency

How urgent is this issue?

What is your timing to accomplish it?

If you don't get a solution to your problem fairly soon, what's the impact on you?

Authority

Who can immediately approve this project?

Who controls the resources required to make it happen?

Who ultimately owns the results of this decision? (By the way, this is the *best question* ever to use in uncovering a decision maker or economic buyer.)

The second step of the sale is handling objections. We've always been taught that the first response we receive is not the actual reason for rejection. Here's how we discover what's really going on. Again, once you've created an environment where emotion is present, the sales dialogue becomes significantly safer for the buyer. As examples:

If we resolve this issue, can we then proceed? (This question respects the buyer by admitting that the objection is a legitimate concern.)

Isn't the likelihood of that outcome occurring fairly low? Please tell me how that bothers you. (This challenges the validity of an objection that might be taking the conversation off course.)

Is that a deal killer? (A brave comment, but a good one to use when things aren't going your way and you are in rapport. It actually asks, "Are you serious?")

The third step is gaining commitment. Three question types are used here to get your buyers to define what success looks like for them, to probe for issues that might undermine the sale at the last minute, then to finalize the sale and find opportunities to upsell, cross-sell, and gain referrals.

Defining Success

How would the operation, in different departments, improve as a result of this work?

What issues would be eliminated with this solution?

How will you quantify or measure the value of this decision?

Preventing Surprises

What might happen that could derail implementing your solution?

How likely is it that we'll be working together?

Do we need to discuss anything else that we haven't yet covered?

Finalizing the Sale

I'll get the details into a proposal document right away. Assuming everything is as we discussed, how soon can we begin?

What would you like to do next?

May I start right now, by preparing you to acquire this solution?

Upselling, Cross-selling, and Referral Opportunities

May I show you some additional options you could find of high value?

Aside from your group, where else might this solution help the organization?

Who do you know outside the organization that I should be talking to as well?

Finally, every sales pro should have five power questions they can use to gain the most potent information needed to close a sale. These questions represent your persuasion power.

RULE 5: SELECT YOUR FIVE POWER QUESTIONS

Based on my twenty-five-plus years of leading and training sales professionals, I've identified the five most popular questions. They are:

1. Could you tell me more or be more specific?

2. How long has that situation been going on, and what has it cost you?

3. What have you done in the past to solve this problem, and how is that working out?

4. How is that problem or situation affecting you personally? How does that make you feel?

5. Have you considered just leaving things the way they are, or what you would do if you couldn't find a solution?

Again, you want to craft your own questions, in your own words. Most important, you must have the discipline and the skill to get your power questions answered.

Categories of Questions

Here are five categories with five questions each. Brainstorm with your team and come up with ten or twelve more in each of these categories.

You'll notice some questions are going to overlap; that's fine. Just make sure, at the end of the day, that you get your most important questions answered.

QUALIFYING

Remember to qualify every prospect early! Your criteria may include finding whether this person matches your perfect prospect profile in terms of budget, access to decision makers (authority), or urgency. Do not ignore the human element here.

One issue everyone struggles with: Can you work with this client? Will the client be open and honest with you? Is the client looking at this relationship as a partnership or are you just a vendor or, worse, a contract worker? Your five questions to ask of clients in order to qualify them are:

- Is this a critical issue that needs urgent attention?

- How do you think we are a good fit?

- Would you share your criteria for identifying the best solution?

- How many other companies have you spoken with?

- Are you solely responsible for this decision, or are others helping?

DISCOVERY

You want to uncover who holds the money (economic buyer), who all the decision makers are, what could go wrong, how much money is available, and whether upselling or cross-selling opportunities exist. If you get resistance at this stage in the process, you might consider backing up and looking at whether this person is truly a qualified prospect. Don't waste time speaking to the wrong person. On the other hand, this is the point when some tough questions need to be answered, so establish and stay in rapport so that you'll get the answers you need.

- Who is the real champion of this initiative?

- Is this project part of your budget, or are the investments to solve this concern under other people's control?

▸ How soon will you decide which solution to use?

▸ What, if anything, could slow up your desire to handle this issue?

▸ As you see the effectiveness of our solutions, can you think of other parts of the organization where, with your introducing us, we would be able to help them?

OBJECTIONS

Primary rule here—don't get defensive! And in spite of the old idea that objections mean there is interest, you want to decide if resistance is really indicative of the buyer's desire to keep you in the dark. In other words, there are honest and dishonest doubters. Your attitude should be to partner with the buyer. When you are working together to help attain company goals or remove roadblocks, you'll move much more smoothly past objections and advance the sale. Notice how each question is prefaced with a softening statement.

▸ Interesting thought. What is the probability of that really happening?

▸ We can probably figure that out together. What do you think we should do?

▸ I was thinking of that as well. Do you think it's even worth worrying about, as we'll be attaining your goals in the end?

▸ Okay, great question. Rather than get into a long conversation now, can the proposal address that concern?

▸ Thank you for sharing that information. Is it a deal killer?

VISION

Your buyers have measures of success. Help them identify and quantify both goals to attain and problems resolved. Quantifying is critically important because many buyers want to understand which metrics will prove they've made a successful decision. Additionally, great sales pros assist to establish outcomes, because often buyers are aware of their *wants* and yet miss some of their *needs*. Work together to identify professional and personal outcomes.

> • What are some ways this solution improves your company's condition?

> • Have you quantified the difference, in the end, of money saved or revenue increased?

> • How does this solution affect you in ways you can measure? What intangible results might you attain?

> • What if you just left things as they are—would it make much difference in the end?

> • What would the perfect solution look like?

GAINING COMMITMENT

You should know this cold, hard selling fact about closing. And you should act upon its truth. The buyer's interest level in you and your solution diminishes the moment you walk out the door. What you don't know is whether interest goes down slowly or whether it plunges like a waterfall to disappear like a drop of water in the middle of a lake. Therefore, the most important thing you should do is to close as quickly as possible.

> • Sounds like we've figured everything out. Shall we start?

> • You can count on receiving my proposal tomorrow. When would you like to have it signed and get me working?

> • What would you like me to do now?

> • It seems like it's in your best interest to get going on this right away. Is there anything else that could keep us from starting?

> • You made a great decision to sit down with me. And it appears we've identified exactly what your issues are and how our solutions eliminate them. What would you like to do now?

In Chapter 12, on objection handling, I encourage you to "find your voice," and the same applies here. Up till now you just blew through a lot of language. Now you want to figure out what language you are most comfortable using and own it for your personal use in the selling field.

▸ ▸ ▸

In summary, the keys to questioning are:

▸ Engage your prospects by connecting with them in a dynamic conversation that emulates a personal friendship or close connection.

▸ Evoke emotion and stay curious!

▸ "Find your voice" and make the questions your own.

▸ Identify and perfect your power questions.

▸ Dig deeper and take your buyers down a path you choose that will lead them to the close.

CHAPTER 12

The Ultimate Objection-Handling Tool

THE PRINCESS BRIDE AND THE PEA . . . We are newly married and it is the first night together in our home. My Princess Bride, Wendy, is getting ready for bed and doesn't notice when . . .

I put a pea under the mattress.

The next morning we are both pretty tired (you'll have to make the logical jump to that point, without storytelling help). When Wendy puts her feet on the floor, griping a bit about getting some rest, I leap out of bed, raise the mattress, and declare, "I know exactly why you're so tired."

I find the pea and hold it up between thumb and forefinger, proof that my wife is a Princess.

She squints at the pea, looks at me, and says, "You're an idiot." Then we start to laugh. The story quickly made its way to Wendy's family and friends and became somewhat immortalized when we started to get Princess and the Pea gifts—books, puzzles, and such. So it's a cute memory, but the point of this story isn't that good practical jokes anticipate the other person's reaction.

There's a lesson here for sale reps:

Great sales professionals can predict the future.

This is totally true. Great sales pros know exactly what *can* happen and so they know what *will* happen. This aptitude is never more evident than it is in handling objections. If you know every form of resistance you can encounter, *and* you have prepared a response for each, you will more readily and more professionally handle anything a buyer throws at you. To accelerate these abilities as a sales professional, I've developed the Ultimate Objection-Handling Tool. It works to manage buyer resistance in three ways:

1. You will identify your top six objections.

2. You will develop potent responses to each of these six objections through three different techniques.

3. You will choose and use those responses that best fit your own personality and communication skills. I strongly encourage all reps to "find their voice" as they increase their ability to persuade buyers. This tool, in fact, will help you to discover what works for you so that you can customize your presentation accordingly.

This chapter then wraps up with seven basic rules you should be willing to adopt whenever you encounter an objection.

Sales managers, executives, and entrepreneurs should look at this chapter as one of the most important briefings they will ever get on the topic of selling. You are going to learn how to build a playbook of responses to your top objections; then, armed with this script, you can significantly shorten the learning curve to master the challenge of handling objections. This method works for both experienced and rookie reps.

Managing Buyer Resistance

This is the part of sales training design where I always have the most fun. It has both short-term and long-term impact for the organization.

IDENTIFYING YOUR TOP SIX OBJECTIONS

Every business has six basic objections that form 98 percent of all the challenges a rep will encounter during a sales call. This first step is best accomplished with your team. Collectively gather all the objections that you hear most frequently. To know which are the toughest, have your team members vote for six they have the most difficulty with. The top six should form the basis of your work in developing influential language to respond to each objection. There are three models I use to develop potent responses.

Common categories of objections generally include:

> ▸ Price that is too high

> ▸ Resistance to change (e.g., new ideas or technology)

> ▸ Existing relationship with competing solution provider

> ▸ Hidden decision maker

> ▸ Requesting literature in order to stall a decision

Some of these protestations are more serious than others. Obviously, if you keep getting the same response, such as "Send me literature," and you can't reach the buyer by phone or e-mail when you follow up, you should be the one resisting—the urge to put a package in the mail, that is.

Here's a quick teaching point on this topic: We train prospects in how to get rid of us. If you continue to send literature when someone is clearly asking for it only to get you off the phone, then you need to stop.

If I could go back in time, once, for any purpose I chose, it wouldn't be to meet an iconic historical figure like Moses or Jesus. It wouldn't be to bet big bucks on some not-a-prayer-of-winning sports upset. And it wouldn't be to buy Apple IPO stock at $22 (it's now well over $300). It would be to track down and strangle the first salesperson who responded to the request to "Send me literature" by saying, "Yeah, sure." How different our selling lives would be if we hadn't committed to training buyers to make us go away by asking for literature!

Now, where were we? Yes, you've gathered all the objections; you can move on to the next step: response models.

DEVELOPING POTENT RESPONSES TO EACH OF THE SIX OBJECTIONS THROUGH THREE DIFFERENT TECHNIQUES

There are three different methods you can use to develop responses to resistance. When you want to build a full playbook of objection-handling responses, then you'll want to go through them all. If you are looking for a quick fix, just pick one and then have the team work through it and see what a difference it makes in their sales dialogues, from that day forward.

This is a pure power play—your sales team will muscle its way through as many responses as everyone can brainstorm. It doesn't matter whether your sales reps' comments are brief or long; just write them all down. The idea is to compile a master list. Your reps can increase their mental flexibility in objection handling by the sheer volume of responses available to them.

Start with the top six objections and take time to work through each one. Here's an example: The buyer says, "Your price is too high." Responses might include:

- What do you mean?

- Compared to what?

- How much did you think it would cost?

- Are your decisions normally driven by investing in the cheapest solution?

- What kind of car do you drive? So you do prefer a quality product? That's just what we provide.

- If our competitors are cheaper, what might that say about them?

- So, would a payment plan help manage bringing in our solution?

You get the idea. This process of collecting possible responses can be great fun. Answers for each objection will range from good to great, from insightful to incredible, from smart to sarcastic. Keep them all.

Remember, the volume of responses serves to help your reps figure out what responses may work best for them individually and what each rep is most comfortable saying.

Be sensitive to the fact that some of the braver responses may only work in two situations: (1) when the seller is in deep rapport with the buyer, or (2) when the seller has no rapport, might be getting a bit desperate, and is almost ready to give up and walk away. The "What kind of car...?" and "If our competitor...?" questions are good examples of responses that take some guts.

BREAKING DOWN LANGUAGE INSIDE THE OBJECTION

This is an advanced language strategy that I encourage everyone to adopt. It focuses on unpacking words within the objection. These are words that, to us, appear to be unclear or without definition.

It's easiest to explain to you by giving an example. You've probably heard, too many times, this objection we've noted previously:

"We're okay with our current situation."

I've chosen this objection as an example because it occurs early in the sales process and, if you don't have an effective response, it can get you stuck or could end the call early.

Look at that phrase again: "We're okay with our current situation." Which words could use some deciphering? In this sentence, you want to scrutinize the words *we, okay,* and *current situation.*

Here's how to craft three questions to respond to three muddled comments within this common objection. Notice after each response how I identify the focal point of the real issue in parentheses.

▸ *Oh, when you say "we," who are you referring to?* (The conversation is going to be about decision makers.)

▸ *Thank you, but can you explain exactly what you mean by "okay"? I'm not sure if that means things are good, great, or whether you're just getting by.* (The conversation is going to be about the buyer's satisfaction with current solutions.)

▸ *When you refer to the "current situation," it's still enough of a concern that we've decided to have this conversation, right? So what is the current situation?* (The conversation is going to be about the buyer's view of the existing issue and its impact on the company.)

The words or phrases you choose to focus on will give you direction for the ensuing conversation. So, by asking who "we" refers to, you'll start to uncover decision-making elements (and individuals) that need to be addressed.

You want to do this kind of language breakdown with each of your top six objections. To show you how many responses there are within the application of this technique, here are a few additional examples where the rep asks for clarity of words within the dialogue:

Objection: We're not sure if we're going to buy right now.

Response: What exactly do you mean by "not sure"?

Alternative Response: When you say "right now," do you have a time frame in mind?

Objection: Your pricing is a concern here.

Response: When you say "concern," do you mean . . . ?

Alternative Response: Pricing in terms of per employee, or total cost? How do you analyze pricing?

Objection: If we did this, we'd have to have some guarantees.

Response: When you say "if," does that mean you are still unsure of our working together?

Alternative Response 1: When you say "if," does that mean you are pretty sure we'll work together, but need some assurances?

Alternative Response 2: Guarantees? Are you referring to . . . ?

You get the idea: Ask for clarity on the words that are not well defined. Do not let buyers use phrases like "We're okay with our current situation" to get rid of you. When people are intentionally vague, they don't see a need to engage you in a dialogue. Your ability to ask great questions (covered in Chapter 11) will help you connect with potential clients.

This is among the unique methodologies I developed for clients who are upgrading their sales training. When I have a roomful of reps who first hear this concept and then start to practice it, I know I've helped elevate them to a level of professionalism they weren't aware existed. You can almost see the lightbulbs going off over their heads as they begin writing their responses to break down the language of each of their top objections. Increased sensitivity to the exact words and phrases a buyer uses is huge for anyone seeking to master communication skills.

In addition, the "organic" nature of this technique means it is useful in personal relationships as well. So see that you practice this technique outside the office, too, and notice how fast and fluidly you begin to use it as you sell.

Let's briefly look at how each rep can customize all the new learning to make it a perfect, individual fit.

Digging Deeper

Your primary reason for responding to objections should be to dig deeper and discover the history behind the comment. This can only happen when you respond with a question.

This technique is a quick and easy way to challenge resistance and find out how serious a buyer is about considering your solution. It isn't for everyone. And it isn't for every situation. But once you understand how to work the language pattern, you'll know when best to apply it.

Your response should follow a three-part pattern set, according to sound psychology principles:

1. State that you are concerned or confused.

2. Explain what it is you are worried about.

3. Ask, "What should we do next?" In other words, challenge the buyer's thinking.

Here are a couple of real-life examples:

Mr. Prospect, I'm a bit confused. You want me to help solve your problem with productivity on the sales team, but you won't share your budget to do this. What should we do now?

Ms. Decision Maker, I'm wondering about something here. We're trying to figure out whether you'll buy our products, but you already have a great relationship with your current vendor. Am I missing something?

You want to practice this approach until you can sound spontaneous and very concerned while, of course, staying upbeat and professional. Striking this balance takes practice, and that practice can pay off in real commissions once you've mastered this language pattern.

Work through each of your six objections and create wording to match the three-part pattern.

Choose and use those responses that best fit your own personality and communication skills.

Finding Your Voice

One of the biggest assets each company has is the collective brainpower of all the sales pros on the team. Yet I rarely meet companies that take advantage of this capacity. Here's proof: At a sales conference, addressing a roomful of real estate brokers and reps, I once performed an exercise to find out how many years of selling experience were represented within the room.

3,782

Do you think within almost 4,000 years of experience you might find every answer to every selling question?

Creative and smart responses to objections, language to land cold-calling appointments, closing tips, and everything else you need exists where you can easily find it! You just have to knock on your neighbor's door and your colleagues can share a cup of sales sugar that'll sweeten your skills and make you more money.

Get smarter, faster and cheaper, by drawing on the collective brain-power of sales pros around you.

Wait, what do you need me for?

Please just stick around for this last piece of the chapter—and then you're on your own.

Now we've created content through our three techniques. We've compiled our "objection-handling playbook." We have pages of words and phrases.

How do you know what *you* should say? Is that response or this one a reflection of *you*? Every rep knows what he would and could say and what he wouldn't or couldn't.

So you want to ask yourself, *Which of these comments would I choose to use?*

Within the wide diversity of personalities in a roomful of reps is more variety in language skills than you could possibly imagine. Some people are visual; some are auditory or tactile. Others are laid back or pushy. There are great listeners and reps who won't shut up.

Often, in training, I'll choose one response to an objection and go around the room asking each salesperson, "Would you say that?" Reactions can cover the spectrum from "Not me" to "Maybe" to "Good one, I like it, yes" to "If I get mad enough about how the call is going . . ."

Each sales professional should be writing down the exact words he is most comfortable using in handling the top six objections. This is what I mean when I say "find your voice."

‣ Be authentic.

‣ Be yourself.

‣ Own the words so that you can use them fluidly and fluently.

That's what great sales pros do. Once you are confident in your ability to predict the future, to smile knowing that you have a great way to handle buyer resistance, you will close more sales.

Finally, here are some basic techniques I encourage all reps to employ when they encounter resistance on a call.

Basic Rules for Handling Objections, or Seven Ways to Stay Out from Behind the Eight Ball

1. *Do not get defensive.* You'll end up begging for understanding and remove yourself from the role of a peer. Ask a question instead of reacting defensively.

2. *Do not respond by telling the prospect how great your products are.* Keep your focus on a health dialogue, rather than feeling a need to brag.

3. *Do respond by agreeing with the buyer's thinking.* But then also ask a question that suggests a counterexample (e.g., "You should probably keep working with your current vendor. You're totally happy with what they've done for you over time, right?")

4. *Do not exhibit excessive enthusiasm.* Nothing damages the initial image of sales reps more. You can be a pro and stay positive without working yourself into a lather.

5. *Do respond with genuine interest.* That means smiling and staying both upbeat and serious.

6. *Be prepared to handle objections.* Come armed with three or five or six responses to every objection you might encounter. Different prospects deserve to be treated differently. This whole chapter is about mental flexibility. How well will you be prepared?

7. *Be prepared to take risks when the sale is in danger.* This is when you have nothing to lose and are mentally prepared to walk away anyway. But remember rule 1 and rule 2: Do not get defensive or pitch product!

One Final Story and Tip for Managing Reps and the Objections They Struggle With

Eric was my sales trainer twenty-five years ago. One day he sat next to me and looked at my call log. This was a print listing of each phone call with the results. (It was the 1980s, so this data wasn't yet available on computer.) But his wisdom was timeless—as you are about to hear. One column on the page was for me to list the objection that ended too many—okay, most—of my calls.

"Dan, do you know why we log the objections?" he asked.

Now, I didn't want to talk about my struggles, so my answer was what psychologists call "deflecting." Casting the attention away from myself, my response went something like, "So the company can create sales training based on the most common forms of resistance?"

Like a good counselor, Eric noticed that I was choosing to ignore my own issues.

"That's a smart and sharp insight," he said. "You probably think that's exactly what I want to hear or perhaps what would impress me. But it's not about the company; it's about you. We want to know exactly what you struggle with. Because once you can handle the top five or six objections, you'll be perceived as an expert by your prospects and within our industry. And that's why you log your objections."

Brilliant thinking on the part of my mentor, and I've never forgotten that conversation. My memory of that exchange is so pure that I can tell you the exact layout of the room and desk where I was sitting.

Now, in my training environments, I make it mandatory for phone reps, in particular, to log objections. Field reps can keep a log as well. It's just that the volume of conversations that occur with phone-based selling makes it easier to identify and coach reps to better handle prospect resistance.

This log can be recorded on paper or formally on the computer—perhaps even in each contact's data record, in a searchable field, so the rep and manager can see at a glance what's troubling the salesperson and slowing up progress toward a successful sale.

▶ ▶ ▶

Decide today to identify your company's top six objections. Encourage the sales team to contribute and own all the content you develop through these models for handling resistance.

Every individual sales pro should then create a personal list of responses. Finally, encourage your reps to also keep the seven rules in mind whenever they do get pushback from buyers.

CHAPTER 13

Strategic Listening

A BUYER REVEALS HIS DECISION-MAKING STRATEGIES. The man walking me into his office was quite fascinated by what I was selling. Our company offered a digital alternative to on-site college recruitment interviews. For about $5,000 a month, his firm could eliminate sending recruiters off to schools around the country.

Problems solved? Cutting quite a few jobs and several hundred thousand dollars in expenses.

Benefits attained? Quicker access to hot hires, and a brand-new digital solution that could position him in the role of a true hero inside the organization.

This senior human resources executive shook my hand and gestured to a chair. I smiled, sat down, and asked, "So, how did you decide to invite me in to meet with you today?"

That was a bit unusual for an opening question, and it took the man a moment to respond.

"Oh, I read your literature thoroughly," he said. "Then I met with my team to decide if it was worth pursuing your solution. They gave me great feedback, and here we are."

What did you just learn from that decision maker's answer?

Here's what I got. His first approach to determining value was to read information. You might say he's visual, and that could be true. His second strategy was to get some form of consensus from respected peers in order to decide to go through the next step. I now knew he was persuaded in two key ways: (1) by absorbing data in print and (2) through external opinions from others he trusted.

Because I'd been listening for these cues, I gained a huge advantage in dealing with this executive. The sale closed for many reasons: The purchase was easy to quantify (there was a great ROI), the need was clearly there, and I was in sync with his "external buyer" style (see Chapter 4).

But what first launched the sale toward its successful conclusion was my ability to listen for that buyer's tendencies.

This piece of the communication equation—listening—is key to setting up great dialogues with everyone in your selling circle: prospects, clients, managers, and support personnel. I'm dedicating a whole chapter to listening, so you'll want to dedicate some serious training time to it as well.

Here's where I get excited about the organic nature and value of training sales pros in all communication skills, including written and verbal dialogues. What you'll learn here has tremendous benefit in your personal life as well as at work. So practice and work on these skills at home, too.

Listening well makes others feel appreciated. It generates intimacy in people who care about one another. Listening to children helps their self-esteem and models how they should act with others. Listening helps others value you in new ways. Think about it. Who doesn't notice when someone is a great listener? With some diligent practice, you can become that great listener.

Great listeners are really following the Golden Rule of communicating: Listen to others as you would have them listen to you. So don't be surprised if your listening and persuasion skills increase together. And here's another key to improving this skill: Tell others (at home and work) that you are developing stronger listening skills. Create accountability toward your improvement in this area by having other people buy into your growth.

Now, let's cover three elements related to improving listening skills:

▶ Understanding why people are poor listeners

▶ Recognizing the keys to good listening

▶ Responding after listening

Of course, we'll use some fun exercises to develop your skills. Again, I encourage you to take this training home. Even share it with family members, and then have them practice with you.

Understanding Why People Are Poor Listeners

Writer Fran Lebowitz once commented, "The opposite of talking isn't listening. The opposite of talking is waiting."

Here's how that happens: We listen at a rate of 600 to 1,000 words per minute. However, we speak at a rate of around 125 to 200 words per minute, with gusts up to 250 words per minute for professional talkers, like TV and radio newscasters.

With this gap between a human's rabbitlike speed of listening and tortoiselike rate of speaking, it's no wonder the mind wanders when a seller begins to talk. So let's look at what makes a poor listener:

▶ Poor listeners think ahead, about their response to the speaker.

▶ They think ahead to what they believe the speaker is going to say (mind-reading should be avoided at all costs, as covered in Chapter 8, on critical language tips).

▶ They multitask during phone conversations (including teleconferences and webinars).

▶ They begin to become defensive, often arguing mentally instead of listening completely.

▶ They become distracted by things outside the speaker (e.g., that book on the shelf, ambient sounds).

▶ They think the speaker is boring (yes, here's one scenario where both parties can share the blame).

> They interrupt (although there is one exception when interrupting the speaker is acceptable, as discussed later).

Recognizing the Keys to Good Listening

Great listeners have great curiosity. This is the foundation upon which we'll build this skill set. When you are curious you won't interrupt, argue, or mentally wander. You'll be totally vested in other people's thought processes as you wonder how they are developing their argument, how they are exploring an idea, how they are expressing themselves. Got curiosity? You'll want to get it today. What else makes for a good listener? Let's take a look. Good listeners:

> Are truly and completely curious about the other person's thought processes.

> Stay mentally positive and neutral about the other person's ideas.

> Mirror body language.

> Maintain good eye contact (at the least, look at the bridge of the nose, not the mouth, because in some cultures looking at the speaker's mouth suggests that you think the person is lying).

> Listen actively by offering verbal signals ("Really?" "Wow, what happened next?" "That's interesting!") as well as nonverbal affirmation, such as nodding and leaning in slightly toward a speaker (known as "attending," which is a very good skill to practice).

> Listen for underlying emotion (see Chapter 9), because responding to the emotion of the situation generates rapport and helps the buyer move toward a buying decision.

> Recognize that it is okay to interrupt if the purpose is to ask for clarity or more detail. This shows true interest and, with a good question, can move the dialogue toward an emotional expression.

> Take notes in a sales setting after asking for permission to do so. (Do you think the speaker is flattered when you begin to immortalize—

at least temporarily—his words in print? How about when you say, "Wow! Hold on, would you repeat that? I want to get every word exactly as you said it.")

▸ Summarize the speaker's comments by speaking in the speaker's dialect (more on this point later in this chapter).

▸ Have outstanding focus because they want to know what's really going on behind the verbal and nonverbal expressions being exhibited by the speaker.

All of these keys to good listening are worth practicing, and we'll use some exercises to help you along in your journey toward listening excellence.

If this topic really fascinates you and you want to truly master listening skills, you'll want to know of Dr. Paul Ekman's work detecting microexpressions in the face (and voice) to determine the emotion the speaker might be attempting to hide. I'm a huge fan of Ekman and have his video training on my desk. It's a fascinating, scientifically sound methodology to understand if a person is misrepresenting the truth. His work was even turned into a hit TV show on Fox, called *Lie to Me*.

While much of Ekman's work is done in conjunction with law enforcement (handcuffed any liars lately?), he is beginning to branch out into the corporate business world. Sales pros should covet any process that can give them an advantage in understanding what's really going on with that person across the table.

Now, let's do a set of exercises (don't worry, they're fun!) to help you increase sensitivity toward other people who are speaking. Your listening skills will be tested and improved in several ways.

Here's Your Homework

▸ This week, focus on that checklist of ten elements you just read.

▸ Sit in a restaurant or an office, even outdoors in the park or at the beach. *Listen.*

▸ Listen and watch for people who are using good listening skills. You want to be like them (in sales and at home).

▸ Monitor conversations that you can use to model excellence in this skill set. Nothing will inspire you faster to adapt these practices to your sales dialogues than to see them in action.

To quote the late Bill Brooks, a brilliant sales tactician and trainer, "Listen people into buying instead of talking your way out of the sale."

Responding–After–Listening Skills

You are done listening, for now.

Here's a story I call "Croaking Frogs and Sales Pros." A few years ago, the Georgia Department of Natural Resources was seeking seventy-five volunteers who would be trained, in advance of tracking season, to listen to frogs so that the state could complete its annual frog survey. Georgia has thirty-one frog species, each with distinctive ribbits and croaks, according to the news report, and the trained surveyors would detect and monitor frog habitats to help officials measure population trends.

How would you like to have a job where listening is your primary role?

Just as one state has thirty-one different frog dialects, each of your buyers uses distinct language choices. These word selections can reveal individual and corporate decision-making strategies. They can point to how aligned (or misaligned) your language choices are to that precious prospect.

Here is a hint about how to increase your listening power: Learn to recognize whether the other person filters information visually or by sound or by touch. Visual speakers might say, "See what I mean?" or "It looks like this. . . ." Auditory speakers might say, "Sounds like . . ." or "Hear what I'm saying?" Kinesthetic/tactile types might say, "We're getting a grip on the issue" or "This can build our performance."

Visual, auditory, and kinesthetic (VAK) is a term used to reference these proven ideas. In psychology, these personal preferences are also called representational (or "rep") systems. They reveal how people process information about their life experience. In a dialogue, you want to repeat back the other person's *exact* "rep" system words to show you understand the individual's concerns and questions.

VAK is older than you might think. Confucius said, "I hear and I forget. I see and I remember. I do and I understand."

I know that we were all taught early in traditional sales training to summarize and restate, using our own words, the comments being made. This approach can create a disconnect if, for example, we offer back visual words to a person who processes information in an auditory fashion.

Here's what I mean. Your buyer says, "I want the company to *hear* what it's like to *sound* confident," and you comment in return, "It *looks* like you want to *show* the company confidence." Notice that it's not the same dialect. In fact, there's a big disconnect. So avoid putting your own spin on the buyer's words.

Hop to it. You don't need to recognize thirty-one croaking conversational styles to improve your listening and your performance. You just need to deal with three. Then your buyers will invite you to spend more time in their habitats. And that leads to more greenbacks in the bank.

Let's summarize the use of these three dialects, so you have specific details on each. You can then get in the proper frame of mind (and tongue) to speak properly for the buyer in front of you.

▸ *Visual Style.* I see what you are saying. That doesn't look quite right. I need to get clear on this idea. The concept is sort of hazy to me right now. I just go blank. That casts some light on the subject. We need a new perspective. That is a colorful example.

▸ *Auditory Style.* That rings a bell. I hear you. It sounds good to me. Listen to this. Everything just suddenly clicked. Tune in to what they're trying to say. I had to ask, myself. That idea has been rattling around in my head for a while.

▸ *Kinesthetic Style.* I've got a good feeling about this project. I need to get a handle on this situation. He needs to get in touch with the flow of the sentiment. You have a solid proposal. We're up against a wall. That's a heavy problem. Can you grasp what needs to be done?

Here's a list of common sensory-based words:

Visual	Auditory	Kinesthetic
see	hear	grasp
look	listen	touch
sight	sound	feeling
clear	resonant	solid
bright	loud	heavy
picture	word	handle
hazy	noisy	rough
brings to light	rings a bell	connects
show	tell	move

So, you've just heard your prospect speak. What exactly have you absorbed, and how will it affect your response? Your ability to pick up as many of these "hidden" clues as possible will affect how well you gain rapport with prospects.

Here, then, are the key things to pay attention to when listening:

▸ *What emotions are being expressed?* And if the speaker's style is clinical or emotionless in expression, what emotions should exist based on the content (i.e., the story or information) shared? It might be hope or joy at the goals that can be attained. There might be frustration or despair at the size of the problem that needs solving. Chapter 9 is dedicated to how to create an emotional context during selling.

▸ *What is the speaker's dialect?* In other words, what do the person's word choices tell you about how this person processes information? Here we want to identify whether the individual is visual ("See what I mean?"), auditory ("Sounds like we could..."), or kinesthetic/tactile ("It feels like the right way to go"). Remember, these dialects are also referred to as representational or "rep" systems.

▸ *What is the speaker's pace?* Pay attention to the pace (speed) of speech, the energy in the voice, the volume, or any other specific manner that reveals the way people discuss the topic in front of them.

Your job now, as you respond, is to match the speaker's emotion, rep system, and other manner of speech. You should also use "You" language before "I" language. This enhances rapport and keeps you totally focused on being other-centered.

So, as an example, consider this response: "Wow, it'll be a huge relief to solve this concern. You've been looking for a way to solve this problem for a while, and my job is to show you how it can happen." This answer respects emotion (frustration), rep system (visual), pace or energy (or speed at which the person communicates), and the "You" focus.

To enhance your skill in hearing the person as clearly as possible, I recommend you practice in your personal and professional life. Ask friends or family members to speak about something they are passionate about—a hobby, a news item, a recent experience. You can then practice a response that feeds back the person's emotion, rep system, and pace, ending with a question for further information (just what you want to do on a sales call). Don't forget the other elements of good listening, too, such as providing verbal and physical affirmation and maintaining good eye contact.

▸   ▸   ▸

To summarize: If you want to improve your listening skills, get and stay curious. Be curious like a child who is fascinated by the world around her, a world that abounds with new colors, sounds, words, and experiences. Listen for word choices, images, and ideas.

Great sales professionals are great listeners. They pick up nuances from buyers that others miss. Practice these skills at home and at work in order to put them into play in front of buyers.

CHAPTER 14

The Opening Strategy for All Sales Calls

A MAN AND HIS WIFE WALK INTO A DENTIST'S OFFICE . . . The man says to the dentist, "Doc, I'm late and in a hurry. I have two buddies sitting out in my car waiting for me. We have a 10:00 a.m. tee time at the best golf course in town and it's 9:30 already, so forget about the anesthetic and just pull the tooth and be done with it."

The dentist thinks to himself, "My goodness, this is surely a very brave man asking to have his tooth pulled without using anything to kill the pain." Then the dentist asks him, "Which tooth is it, sir?"

The man turns to his wife and says, "Open your mouth, honey, and show him."

Funny story, but can you really control another person? More precisely for sales pros, can you control a buyer? One idea was pounded into me when I grew up in selling: You must control the sale.

Here's the bad news about that old-school thinking: You *can't* control the sale. But there's good news, too: You *can* take charge of the sale. There is a world of difference here.

You take charge by gaining agreement on the steps you and the buyer will take as you explore the possibility of working together. This strategy of gaining agreement to begin the selling process with your buyer is the single best indicator of sales skill, or talent, I've ever encountered. It's also the single most critical strategy I teach in sales training.

See, too much emphasis is placed on closing. In fact, if you don't open strongly enough, you'll never get close to the close. You must have a method for taking charge of the buyer/seller interaction, gaining agreement as to how the two of you will "play the game" and how the conversation will end.

A Psychologically Sound Strategy to Opening Sales Calls

Eric Berne, whose social psychology theory formed the basis of Transactional Analysis, defined an agreement as a "specific commitment, with a well-defined course of action." This whole field of psychology is founded on a contractual approach to each doctor/patient dialogue. Berne further describes a contract as "an explicit bilateral commitment to a well-defined course of action," which means that all parties need to agree:

- Why they want to do something

- With whom they'll deal

- What they are going to do

- By when it will be done

- What (if any) fees, payment, or exchanges there will be

Sounds a lot like all the information we want on the table to complete and close a sales call, doesn't it?

Contracts need to be framed in positive words that make clear what you want to achieve, rather than what you don't want. When we look through a negative lens, we focus too much on failure. As you look at the examples that follow, and create your own agreements, try to craft them around positive words.

Berne also notes that contracts need to be measurable, manageable, and motivational. Measurable means that the goals need to be tangible, and that all parties involved in the contract will be able to say in advance how they will know when the goal has been achieved. The goal must be specific and behavioral and clearly defined. The contract also needs to be manageable and feasible for all those concerned.

Enough heavy learning for now. Let's make it practical for the sales pro. Great sales pros use their own *behavioral contracts* (BCs). This is the selling term I use to embody where sound psychology intersects sound selling. Successful sales reps look at an agreement as a three-step process:

1. Gain time commitment.

2. Establish the rules of communication.

3. Set a purpose or goal.

Let's review each of these steps and learn how to build them into your prospect interactions. But first, let me give you some quantifiable reasons that validate the potency of this strategy.

A few years ago, I was asked to redesign a sales training program for a national financial services firm you'd probably recognize. The redesign project was to add the latest best practices as well as my own influence and persuasion strategies to the company's two-day sales training experience.

We measured, then modeled, the company's top rep, Steve, who was using his own form of a BC to begin his conversations with buyers. His numbers were a bit intimidating to the firm's average reps.

The average salesperson spent twelve and a half hours with a prospect over the course of several meetings before the buyers bought or went away. But Steve gained agreement right away and then determined within *thirty-seven minutes* whether the buyers were worth his time. He then pursued them or graciously said good-bye (you'll learn how to do that as well). And the results:

▸ The average salesperson closed 15 percent of his prospects.

▸ Steve closed 76 percent of those with whom he engaged beyond the thirty-seven minutes.

Does a behavioral contract (BC) really work? I could give you dozens more personal sales stories, not just my own (though there are plenty there), to show it does work. Here is one of my favorites:

Dave was invited to attend one of my two-day training events but had an appointment the first afternoon that he could not reschedule. That first morning he created his BC, and at lunchtime he left for his sales call. The next morning, Dave walked up to me before class beaming a huge smile. I asked how the call went.

He said, "I'm sitting opposite my prospect in those awkward first moments of a sales call. He knows I'm there to sell him. I know he's here to measure my honesty, my pushiness, my products—you know, all the things prospects are doing while they're also trying to get the best deal, should they buy. So I did the behavioral contract, my first time ever, and when I said that we were basically there to figure out whether we'd work together, the tension just drained out of his face. His defenses dropped and our dialogue was totally safe for both of us. I was on the first call of my life where I didn't feel pressured to sell and he obviously didn't feel pressured to buy. This BC really works."

Dave went on to say that he got the second appointment scheduled—a solid use of a smart strategy by a sales pro.

By the way, I always require the sales pros I train to carry their BC with them, during the day and into classes. There's nothing more important in their arsenal.

Now, let's review the three-step behavioral contract agreement in detail.

1. *Gain time commitment.* Here you want to revisit the amount of time agreed upon when the meeting was set up.

2. *Establish the rules of communication.* Then you ask permission to have an open, honest discussion. This step includes (as you will see) getting permission to ask lots of questions.

3. *Set a purpose or goal.* Finally, you gain agreement that the purpose of this meeting is simply to determine if you and the buyer should be working together. In other words, let's recognize how this meeting is going to end. Do you want to schedule a second meeting or just part ways?

Once the prospect agrees to these three elements of your BC, you'll thank him and then open with a leading question.

Here are three examples. The last one (Example C) represents the boldest set of language choices. The key here is to form your own BC. You are to "find your voice" and make the words you choose a reflection of your personality. That's why you want to share your BC with others on the sales team, too. It'll help all of your sales reps land on language they feel most comfortable using.

Also, notice that in all three of the sample dialogues, the sales pro makes sure the prospect confirms an understanding and *agrees* to each step.

EXAMPLE A

The saleperson with a very conversational style nonetheless starts off by confirming the time commitment and the rules of the communication, as follows:

"You said on the phone that we'd have forty-five minutes together. Is that still good? Great. And is it okay for us to set an objective or outcome for this time? Good. Let's do it.

"You'll want some questions answered and I will, too. So let's just be candid with each other, and if it looks like what you and I are trying to accomplish are just not in sync, will you please tell me that this doesn't seem like a fit? And if I realize that I can't help you, I'll tell you right away, as your time is precious. Okay?

"Please, don't worry about hurting my feelings. Just be candid, so I don't get the wrong signal and hound your e-mail and voice mail while you try to figure out a way to ignore me."

The next part of the dialogue establishes how the meeting will end:

"So, at the end of our meeting together, a couple things can happen: We agree that we're not going to work together and say good-bye. Or we realize we need another meeting because you need to review matters with someone else, or I need to get some figures to you or something similar. Should we need to meet again, we'll simply set the appointment before I go. That way we can handle this issue quickly.

"If you are undecided about what to do next, it probably means you're not comfortable with our solutions and we'll assume that we're not going to work together. I just want to be professional about managing our time. And again, please be candid as soon as you figure out whether we can work together or should go our separate ways. Is that okay with you? Great, thank you.

"Now, what's the biggest concern you wanted to address during our time today?" (*Or,* "What's the No. 1 reason you invited me in today?")

EXAMPLE B

The dialogue spoken here is more direct (i.e., less chatty) than in Example A:

"We're trying to figure out if this relationship is a match. At the end of our meeting together, three things can happen.

"First, we figure out that we're good for each other and determine our next step to begin working together. Second, we might agree that we're not going to work together and say good-bye. Or, third, we realize that we need another meeting because you need to review matters with someone else or I need to get some figures or additional information to you. Should we need to meet again, we'll simply set the appointment before I go. That way we can treat this issue quickly.

"If, after our forty-five minutes together, you are undecided about what to do next, it probably means you're not comfortable with what we offer, or our solutions, and we'll assume that we're not going to work together.

"Does that set a good framework for our conversation? Good. Now, what's the biggest concern you wanted to address during our time today?"

EXAMPLE C

This dialogue is the boldest approach:

"How about I take a few minutes and explain how I work. Because this might be a very short meeting. I'm certain you have questions for me, and I have questions for you. Typically, I take some time to get a picture of who you are. Some questions might be about the personal impact of this decision. Will you be okay with that?

"The purpose of this meeting is simply to determine if we should have a second meeting.

"You might discover before I do that a second meeting isn't necessary. Will you be nice enough to tell me? On the other hand, if I discover that before you do, I'm going to be very candid with you and let you know. Fair enough?

"When I'm working with serious clients like yourselves—you are serious, aren't you?—I usually take two to three meetings. By the end of that time, some of my clients look at me and say, 'No, this is not for me,' which, by the way, is perfectly okay with me. I'll just close your file and keep you on our mailing list. On the other hand, if you say, 'Yes, this program is for me,' we'll go ahead with the paperwork. By the end of the third meeting, if you still have to think about it, I can assure you this program isn't for you, so please just tell me *no* outright, okay?

"Great, let's get started. . . ."

The Big Behavioral Contract Bonus

There are basically only four ways a sales call can end. Let's look at their value to us as sales pros.

1. *The prospect says* yes. This outcome is a good thing, of course, because you have acquired a new client!

2. *The prospect says* no. Is hearing a *no* a good thing? Yes, it is! You are not going to lie in bed at night wondering if that person could buy from your business. Great sales pros don't chase poor prospects. You can cycle back to this person later, but for now you are done and have moved on to investing time in the well-qualified, perfect prospect.

3. *You set the next appointment.* Trick question: Is "Call me next Thursday" an appointment? No! What if the prospect says, "Call me next Thursday afternoon"? No! How about, "Call me next Thursday at 2:00 p.m."? Yes, you have set an appointment.

Even then, if you've ever had a prospect blow off an appointment, you know you need to plan for that possibility. So, for example, you should ask a follow-up question: "Mr./Ms. Prospect, what shall we do if I can't reach you at 2:00 p.m.?" The response might be, "Call my assistant, or try a half hour later." Plan for your surprises, and you won't have any.

4. *The prospect wants to "think it over."* Is thinking it over a good thing? No! It is the single worst phrase anyone in selling can hear. Your bonus for using the behavioral contract is that you virtually eliminate this dreaded response. If someone says, "I'd like to think about it a bit," you gently remind the person that the agreed goal/outcome/purpose of today's conversation was to get each other's questions asked and answered, then to determine if that's enough to say *yes* or *no* or to set another appointment. A healthy agreement permanently eradicates Think It Over Syndrome from your sales life. Now, is *that* a good thing? Yes!

To further reinforce the value of a strong opening strategy as a key strength to supplement closing skills, look at this double-axis grid. You get the picture.

Sales pros who open with agreement.

	STRONG	OPENING SKILLS	WEAK
STRONG CLOSING SKILLS	World-Class Sales Pro		Disqualifies Self from Opportunity
WEAK	Friendly, But Gets No Decision		Unemployed

The Buyer's Perspective

Salespeople often walk into a meeting with their personal agenda (Sell now!) as the primary goal. But let's consider the buyer's perspective for a moment, too. When someone comes in showing respect for my time and professionally sets an agenda, I know I can work with this person. When the meeting ends with closure and a solid understanding of the status of the relationship, as well as the next steps, I have had a most unusual and delightfully memorable experience.

That's why I'd like to again point out that opening strong might be the most valuable piece of the sales training puzzle I've taught over the last twenty-five years. It is well worth the rep's time and energy to practice the behavioral contract strategy.

▸ ▸ ▸

In summary: The opening strategy for all sales calls is the behavioral contract. This is a solid way to take charge of a sales call and to gain agreement from the buyer about expectations. It's a truly professional way to run a meeting. And it doesn't allow for the opportunity of a "Think it over" request from the buyer. While the behavioral contract takes some effort to adopt—it does require that you craft an agreement in your own words and then settle on an approach you can feel comfortable with—it might be the most valuable strategy a salesperson can use to initiate every sales call. You really can take charge of a sales dialogue, you can set expectations, you can help the buyer set some clear next steps. But it takes practice being able to comfortably and casually offer the behavioral contract as the opening to each of your sales calls.

CHAPTER 15

How to Be Funny: Humor for Sales Pros

THE FUNNIER YOU ARE, THE MORE YOU GET PAID. This chapter is literally a workshop on being funny. You can pay attention or continue to bore prospects, friends, and family to the point where they'll ignore you. (*Psst.* Wonder why people like watching TV with you? It's because then they don't have to carry on a conversation.)

You're thinking, "Humor skills training, in an influence book?" Why not? George Carlin introduced the language tips in Chapter 8. I've collected more than 600 hilarious selling blunders, and I serve my readership with as much wit as wisdom.

There's an adage in the professional speaking world that the funnier you are the more you get paid. Since the theme of this book is that influence increases income, we'll add humor to the persuasion equation.

So, do you like hanging out with funny people? Do you think entertaining sales professionals distinguish themselves from others? Do you want to help make others love your company? Getting people to laugh is a rush!

In this chapter I'll teach you how to cultivate a fun and funny persona—both in print and in person. In fact, you may want to read it just for the entertaining examples while you figure out how to find your voice and make these strategies your own. Just model my techniques and see how quickly you attract more attention and better responses from prospects, plus deeper relationships with existing clients. Once you begin to adapt some of these ideas to your own life, people will read and respond to more of your e-mails and letters.

Even if you are a naturally funny guy or gal, you can still benefit from this chapter. Here are your three steps:

1. Absorb funny.

2. Write funny.

3. Speak funny.

Absorb Funny

As a serious athlete, I never put steroids into my body, but you can create a steroid effect on your sense of humor by reading funny material. You can get totally powered up by absorbing jokes, witty thoughts, and comic-centered content. Let's look at reading resources as well as video and audio options that are on tap.

My personal favorite three humor books are:

> *Napalm & Silly Putty* by George Carlin

> *Comedy Writing Secrets* by Mel Helitzer and Mark Shatz

> *I Am America* by Stephen Colbert

Here's why (and I do recognize your sense of humor might mean your style or preference is different). Carlin was brilliant with words. His stand-up work over three decades showed the world that he was a master at tickling the brains, ears, and funny bones of his audience. Look at his take on sports from *Napalm & Silly Putty:*

To my way of thinking there are really only three sports: baseball, basketball, and football. Everything else is either a game or an activity.

Soccer. Soccer is not a sport because you can't use your arms. Anything where you can't use your arms can't be a sport. Tap dancing isn't a sport. I rest my case.

Swimming. Swimming isn't a sport. Swimming is a way to keep from drowning. That's just common sense.

Sailing isn't a sport. Sailing is a way to get somewhere. Riding the bus isn't a sport, why the f__k should sailing be a sport?

Bowling. Bowling isn't a sport because you have to rent shoes. Don't forget, these are my rules. I make 'em up.

Comedy Writing Secrets is a book that will really raise your humor IQ. It gives you the secret codes to drawing humor out of specific situations, stories, even phrases. When you are able to mentally break down how jokes are built, you'll significantly increase your ability to craft your own. Eventually, you'll be able to do it spontaneously—even if it's finding the perfect moment to share a joke that's already been written.

This happened to me in the days leading up to my writing this chapter, when I was keynoting a sales conference. Someone made a comment that one of the reps had attended three funerals in the past week. I ad-libbed, "Yes, I was talking to Shel before we started and he said he's confused by obituaries in the newspaper. Wonders why people always die in alphabetical order." Got a huge laugh, even though it's an old joke.

Similar to *Comedy Writing Secrets* are three other resources that I recommend. Doug Stevenson's *Get More Laughs,* available on CD (story-telling-in-business.com), reveals twenty-nine techniques to get more laughs. Humor Mall (humormall.com) is the website founded by John Cantu, who, before his death, coached stand-up wannabes and wrote humorous greeting cards. Finally, Dave Glickman's *Punchline Your Bottom Line* is written by a former owner of comedy clubs who is absolutely hilarious in person and while performing. He helps speakers punch up their material by embedding funny lines throughout their talks.

These five resources, in particular, demonstrate the inner workings, the structure behind the comedy. I'm also a big fan of Dave Barry's work, and after inundating myself with these comedy-training tools, I could see exactly how Barry creates humor in his work.

Colbert's *I Am America* is simply a written work of art (visually and verbally funny) that reveals plenty of great material from one of the top TV humorists and his comedy-writing team. Jon Stewart of *The Daily Show* has produced similar content in his books. And one of my favorite books with punch line after punch line is *The Best of the Show: A Classic Collection of Wit and Wisdom* by Bill Scheft. Scheft was a writer for David Letterman. This book might be a bit hard to find, but worth poring over to discover lots of humor tricks. There are hundreds of pages of jokes inspired by news items from the world of sports. Because the news items are circa the early 2000s, the content is somewhat dated, but still very, very funny and a great tutorial for our purposes.

Watch the late-night TV hosts when you can. Classic *Saturday Night Live* DVDs, available at your local library, can inspire you to laugh and absorb strategies as well. Watch them on your TV or laptop. Good stand-up comedians (even those, like Carlin, who have potty mouths) are worth your viewing time. Here's an important thought: If you spend tons of time in front of that expensive flat-screen HDTV, why not use it to increase a skill set that can make you laugh, make you funnier, and eventually make you more money?

Last, another way to absorb funny is to download plenty of material at iTunes or Amazon. So listen in your car, on the plane, during downtime. Find sources that you enjoy, that reflect your personality and growing sense of humor, and you'll increase your laugh potential.

It gets easier from here, because my "tricks to writing funny" are much simpler than you could ever imagine.

Write Funny

Everyone is communicating by e-mail these days. Each time you "touch" a prospect this way, you have a chance to become memorable or lost in the in-box. Which will you choose? Okay, it's a dumb question, but not as dumb as answering "I want memorable!" then doing nothing. The purpose of this book is to change your behavior. Writing funny is one of the easiest things to learn. I use this technique with e-mails, social media posts, and my blogs.

Here's what you'll do. You want to send your e-mails with the subject line, "Melissa [unless your prospect's name is Mark], I was thinking of you. . . ."

That will get read. That will move your prospect to the body of the e-mail, where you'll continue: "I was reading this article [or joke, personal story, or news item] and thought you should see this." Then you'll copy or create something entertaining. Using the PET—personal, emotional, trainable—storytelling model (see Chapter 10), you'll create some emotional context, then give a final thought or a call to action (depending on whether you just want to connect or want another next step).

Here's an example. I sent this personal story to a senior sales executive to get him to consider having me train his team:

Subject: Jim, I was thinking of you today. . . .

So, Jim, are you ready for Valentine's Day? I remembered this dumb mistake and thought it would give you a laugh, maybe something to share around the office.

I'm newly married and Valentine's Day is creeping up. What do I do? Well, everything I stand for in selling is about standing out from everyone else.

I thought everyone gets roses, so I'll be different and get something unique. My Princess Bride will be overjoyed at my creativity.

But what would I do? Then it hit me. Remember Venus-- Goddess of Love from mythology? I'll do something related to Venus.

So I got her a plant--a Venus flytrap.

You know, they're the little plants that slam shut on insects when they crawl into them. Digestive juices begin to dissolve the little bugs, which end up as plant food.

I felt bad at the store buying them, because they were so inexpensive. But I felt better by getting her two.

Gotta be honest, it didn't go over very well. But I realized later what I was doing was perfect from a salesperson's perspective. It just wasn't the wisest thing to do with my wife.

Our job is to distinguish ourselves from everyone else who sells. So I resisted roses because I wanted to stand out in my giftgiving.

See, I'd already "sold" my bride on me. She "bought" the day she said *yes* to "Will you marry me?" And she proved there was no buyer's remorse when she said "I do."

But your sales professionals still have to distinguish themselves from other sales reps. How are you doing that?

Let's set a time to talk.

Dan

There's the formula. It's that simple. Here's another example where I use a joke to set up a memorable moment:

Subject: Janet, I was thinking of you today. . . .

I was reading some George Carlin (very funny comedian) and this line perfectly frames the issue we discussed: *Sometimes on a rainy day I sit around and weed the losers out of my address book.*

Remember our talk on the No. 1 problem that sales pros face? Chasing poor prospects. Carlin's pointing out that this concept has value in our personal lives as well.

Let's set a time to talk about eliminating that problem by building that qualifying/disqualifying strategy into your training.

Best,
Dan

You get the idea. Now, where do you get the content? Here is a list of bizarre, funny, and fascinating websites you can use for starters:

Brainmail lists unusual statistics, developments in products, and ideas from around the world. For example, it was one of the first sources reporting on the development of transparent concrete, used for building security barriers as well as increasing access to sunlight to reduce energy costs. (My message tie-in was personal transparency.) Another favorite was the revelation of the European company Sky Sails (www.skysails.info/), whose brilliant idea is to use gigantic kites on ships to supplement and reduce fuel costs by using wind power. (My tie-in: What are you doing to increase efficiency in your sales day, and your ability to generate leads and close faster?) Subscribe to the monthly edition at brainmail.nowandnext.com.

The Onion (www.TheOnion.com) is the funniest site on the Internet that parodies news across the planet. There are daily and weekly updates, including audio and video clips. This is a professionally produced humor site, with nothing else like it anywhere.

Odd news sites are fun for picking up quirky stories that people enjoy. Look into:

- NewsoftheWeird.com
- ThisisTrue.com
- Weird News on MSNBC (www.msnbc.msn.com/id/4429957)

Discovery News (news.discovery.com) and *American Scientist* (www.americanscientist.org/science) are two science resources with some fascinating material as well. I sent out an e-mail on energy and efficiency after I read an article on a gas turbine engine that can fit on a quarter and runs for fifteen to twenty hours! It could replace laptop batteries. Lots of great content here.

On This Day in History (www.on-this-day.com) will inspire anyone who wants a tie-in to a historic event, a celebrity birthday, or something similar.

Chase's Calendar of Events is even better, or just a bit different. Available in a print and online version from McGraw-Hill Professional (www.mhprofessional.com/category/?cat=3), it is a comprehensive reference listing of historical information as well as special "days" like National Grandparents' Day.

Despair.com is a parody site with incredibly funny visuals that take a shot at all the inspirational and motivational pictures that many managers post in their offices. These "demotivators" are presented with superb graphics and sarcastic messages, like my favorite top 10:

1. *Apathy.* If we don't take care of the customer, maybe they'll stop bugging us.

2. *Customer Care.* If we really care for the customer we'd send them somewhere better.

3. *Defeat.* For every winner, there are dozens of losers. Odds are you're one of them.

4. *Do It Later.* The early worm is for the birds.

5. *Leaders.* Leaders are like eagles. We don't have either of them here.

6. *Meetings.* None of us is as dumb as all of us.

7. *Mistakes.* It could be that the purpose of your life is only to serve as a warning to others.

8. *Procrastination.* Hard work often pays off after time, but laziness always pays off now.

9. *Whining.* If you expect to score points by whining, join a European soccer team.

10. *Worth.* Just because you're necessary doesn't mean you're important.

Do you have a favorite cartoon? Look it up online as well. You can also use printed materials to uncover some funny ideas. I have a wall lined with humor books, including plenty of joke books. If you want some best of the best jokes, look at anything by Judy Brown. She collects the funniest lines from today's top stand-up comedians.

Here's a joke I told to teach a sales lesson related to how we progress in our careers:

> An amateur photographer was invited to a dinner and brought a few photographs. The host looked at them and commented, "These are very good. You must have an excellent camera."
>
> Later in the evening, as the photographer was leaving, he turned to the host and said, "That was a delicious meal. You must have some excellent pots."

Ouch, enough with the cheap shots. But you get the point. Who or what gets credit for your performance? It might be you—your skills, behavior, and persuasiveness. But there's probably more. . . .

It's your training.

And your mentors.

And your products.

And your company.

And the books you've read, audios you've heard, conferences you've attended, and more.

Turn a joke into a teaching moment and you'll connect better with your buyers.

How about sending cards and letters? I have some outstanding strategies here as well. I use a service that allows me to customize greeting cards to send out to prospects. I design the concept and pay an artist to create a cover. The process is easy and quick and the service manages printing and mailing through the post office, although you can customize images, pictures, and the messages on your computer and mail it from there, too, very inexpensively.

One image I use a great deal is the high-quality, colorful cover of my *Sales Comic* book. It shows two sales managers who are talking on the phone; one asks, "So how many salespeople work for you?" The other replies, "About half of them."

This is a perfect lead-in to a laugh and the question: Are your salespeople in need of great sales training?

You can read about this service, then start using it at this website: www.LeadGenerationGenius.com.

I've also developed a video game for salespeople, *Revenge of the Reps.* This high-quality, three-level Flash game lets you tear into evil prospects who put you off with objections like:

- I won't buy from you or your descendants.

- Lower your price to match your IQ.

- Salespeople should be licensed and leashed.

- I was frightened by a salesman at birth.

- I hate salesmen; my ex-husband was one.

- I'd love to see you—on the cover of a milk carton.

You get the picture. If you are interested in the game, e-mail me (Dan@GotInfluenceInc.com) and I'll reply with a copy!

You now have plenty of ways and reasons to write funny in your e-mail, online, and in other communications. Let's look next at your actual presentations and how to add humor to your live interactions with prospects.

Speak Funny

Any reading or training you might acquire on speaking will tell you how critical those first few minutes are in front of your audience.

The bizarre, funny, and fascinating can be used as a basis for opening a sales call or group presentation, even for a speech meant to generate awareness and leads at a conference or trade show. I often open with a variety of news items, science facts, and personal stories, plus a joke or a funny list. Here are two examples. Read through them to get a flavor for how to grab attention from the first moment you interact with an audience of one or many. At the end of each example (in parentheses), I show where the entertaining content turns into a sales pitch or teaching moment.

DEATH SENTENCE FOR DESTROYING SALES?

Shijiazhuang, China (CNN)—The former chairwoman of China's Sanlu dairy was sentenced to life in prison and three others received death sentences Thursday in a tainted milk scandal that killed at least 6 infants and sickened nearly 300,000 others.

Maybe we're too easy on ourselves and our sales teams when they don't produce.

(That's my jumping off point to talk about the need to be highly productive during the day; that is, the value of reps focusing on income-producing behavior, not administrative work, whenever they have access to prospects.)

WRONG-WAY DRIVER . . .

As a senior citizen is driving down the freeway, his cell phone rings. Answering, he hears his wife's voice urgently warning him, "Herman, I just heard on the news that there's a car going the wrong way on Interstate 280. Please be careful!"

"It's not just one car, honey," says Herman. "It's hundreds of them!"

Hey, sales executives . . . how well have you mapped out the direction of each key piece of your sales professional's working life? How about your lead-generation sources, combined with the ability to qualify quickly? Great persuasion skills? An ability to smoothly and confidently deal with any objection?

(This starts a sales call on what great sales training focuses on and what can be left out.)

Could you open a presentation with these remarks? It might be too much of a risk for you. Then again, now might be the time to take a few risks and see what better return you get when closing ratios go up.

For more details on openings, spend some time with the material in Chapter 10, on the persuasive power of storytelling in sales.

Here are some other ways to improve the impact of your presentations. Remember, not all of these ideas are appropriate for a serious sales call, but you'll find opportunities to use them to spice up some of your other presentations.

▸ *License movie clips.* I love video clips. And I use them legally. I have a license with the Movie Picture Licensing Corporation (MPLC) to employ video clips in all my presentations, including training and keynotes. Most recently I'm using the scene from *The Blues Brothers*, that I describe in Chapter 7. The clip is perfect for a training program on the psychology of excuses, as Jake kneels, clasps his hands in prayer, and begs his ex-fiancée to believe that it wasn't his fault that he jilted her that day he left her at the altar.

When I first started looking at using video clips it was ridiculously expensive. Years ago I called to find out what it would cost to use a wild sword-fighting scene from *The Princess Bride*. In the scene the two opponents banter, withholding and revealing information to each other as they dance and clash over rocky terrain. The clip is a perfect metaphor for buyers vs. sellers. But, it was $1,500 for me to use it one time.

I've since made an arrangement with Sal Laudicina, the president of MPLC. Business professionals who want an inexpensive way to license video clips can begin using this entertaining technique to gain attention and increase prospects' interest in their solutions: www.InfluenceWith Videos.com.

There are plenty of other ways to spice up your presentations.

▸ *Find some props.* I've used a Barbie doll with pins sticking out of her as a voodoo doll to represent bad prospects who waste our time and frustrate us. (My daughter wasn't happy when I brought that doll home from a sales call; now I have to ask permission to take her toys.) I'll say to a sales team, "Who would you hurt and where would you stick the pins?" Good visual, good laughs.

I once had very cheap logo watches made. These digital toys were so sensitive to static electricity that they'd stop working when you walked on carpet. I solved that problem by giving them out and saying, "These are really cheap. Our guarantee is, if they break on you, send them back and we'll dispose of them properly." Lemon into lemonade, right?

I once found an advertisement in an airline magazine for a negotiating seminar by Dr. Chester Karrass. This guy's company has 650 seminars each year all over the globe. They are designed basically to teach buyers how to beat up salespeople on price. I held it up and said, "Anyone seen this in their airplane seat pocket?" Lots of nodding heads. "Is it just a coincidence that, in the same location, salespeople find this . . . ?" And I hold up a barf bag, to great laughter.

I've given away my *Sales Comic* book, video games, and other products. I've purchased weird jerky made from alligator, ostrich, boar, and kangaroo to share with people ("Did you get enough to eat earlier?"). Do anything that keeps you from standing in one place and boring everyone. The jokes are there, waiting for you to discover them and share them with your audience.

▸ ▸ ▸

Bottom line on punch lines: This chapter makes me think that I probably need to write a book on the practical jokes I've pulled on people during my sales career. You'll have to contact me directly when you want some of those stories (or if you're liking the thought of taking action and pulling some pranks and want some ideas).

Keep this in mind, though: Like it or not, people label one another. You can be the really smart sales pro or the persistent sales pro or the experienced sales pro. It's nice when people begin to distinguish you from other sellers by saying, "That guy is really funny," or at least "fun to be with." Do your homework: Absorb funny, write funny, and speak funny.

CHAPTER 16

Potent Communication Skills

UH-OH . . . ACTUARIES IN THE AUDIENCE! I was invited to do my *Secret Language of Influence* program on communication skills in one of my favorite cities, San Diego.

My audience was . . . actuaries!

For those unfamiliar with these financial "scientists," actuaries evaluate past and present insurance statistics to estimate future financial risks. On the basis of their findings, they calculate insurance premium rates and also design or modify policies to keep their companies profitable and competitive.

These men and women *love* mathematics, like those two people you remember from high school (wait, one of them hated math but was good at taking tests). Actuaries go through an insane litany of tests, over the course of a decade, in order to have the privilege to work with spreadsheets all day long.

These people are brilliant and great at what they do. It's pretty easy to quantify their value to the organization; they save significant money, so in that respect they are much like sales pros.

However, an actuary is about as internal a human being as you will ever meet. So much so that many people don't consider actuaries human. Okay, that's an actuary joke I was told. They have their own jokes, just like lawyers. The best joke I heard (three different actuaries were brave enough to come up to me, a stranger, and share it) is this one: "How do you know you've met a gregarious actuary? When talking to you, he's looking at your feet, instead of his."

You get the picture. So, when an executive from this organization contacted me to speak, she said, "We're actuaries, we need help with communication skills. Will you come to San Diego?" I live in Chicago; it was winter when she called. How would you have responded?

When the training ended, I walked to the door to say good-bye to 100 attendees. There are plenty of thank-yous and nice comments like, "I can really use this information," however . . .

Not one person shook my hand.

People actually held on to their opposite wrist when they spoke to me, as if pinning their arm to their stomach would send a clear signal to both of us that a handshake wasn't happening. It's very strange to greet 100 people without a single handshake, when there are no worries about bird flu, swine flu, or leprosy.

I mentioned it to a couple of the organization's executives—not to be rude or imply I was upset—but just to make an observation about how well we do or do not connect with others. "We're actuaries, we don't know how to connect. That's exactly why we invited you in," one of them said.

How well do you connect with others? How well does your selling team connect? Connecting covers a lot of areas in the selling life. We need to better engage buyers through our written and verbal skills.

Written Skills

Here's a story by a financial planner named Larry that illustrates why written communications are critical to a sale.

OBEDIENT PROSPECTS CLOSE THEMSELVES

As a certified financial planner I was proud to say I could sell myself without ever mentioning the "insurance" word. I made great money from offering policies to match my clients' portfolios.

When I got an appointment, I would mail a letter describing what our discussion would be like. Most important, I included a blank chart where prospects could write down all assets and liabilities, as well as coverage they had (or didn't).

So a two-and-a-half-hour drive to meet and assess the financial needs of a well-to-do young couple was going to be worth the trip. Of course, the tricky part is getting your prospect to do that prework for you. In fact, potential clients who gather paperwork and crunch numbers before a meeting have qualified themselves as very hot prospects.

This couple shared that they had done exactly as I'd requested! They had organized an incredibly detailed display of information on their assets and liabilities.

"Wow," I said, "thank you for taking the time to create this picture of your finances. It will help us structure a plan to manage your money for the short term and long haul." I was setting them up for the fact that they were probably underinsured and missing some coverage as well.

The man and his wife both broke into broad smiles. "This was a great exercise. We had no idea of the scope of our family finances. In fact, we noticed several places on the form were blank." He paused, leaned in, and pointed to some large numbers on his personal balance sheet. . . .

"So to make your job easier, we had someone come over last night and we bought a bunch of insurance."

I thought I would cry.

Poor Larry. His written communication just didn't communicate very well. He not only didn't influence his buyers to buy, he influenced them to buy elsewhere! Larry's letter should have clearly persuaded the prospect not to make any decisions until they sat down with him. A clear understanding of roles would have saved Larry both the time and the tears.

How well do you design your written communications? That would include both e-mail and letters.

Since much of the literature that salespeople use is designed by marketing, I'll be brief and to the point: To exert influence with the written word, you must make a professional impression. Your personal writing should incorporate the following three elements:

 ▶ Be buyer-centered.

 ▶ Emphasize time sensitivity.

 ▶ Include a call to action.

BE "YOU" FOCUSED, RATHER THAN "WE" FOCUSED

Look how big we are! Here's how long we've been around! This is our plant overseas! We can make you happy when you buy from us!

These statements are typical of too much copywriting today. The subject of each sentence is the sender, the salesperson. The subject of each sentence should be the buyer, the person with the money.

Review and rewrite all of your e-mail and letters and invert the sentence structure to speak directly to the person reading it.

My favorite authority who coaches this technique is Jerry Weissman, author of *Presenting to Win*. Jerry personally advises major corporate executives how to present to potential shareholders when their companies are going public. In other words, he is helping people sell hundreds of millions of dollars of stock. You should own his book; I bought it to see how I might better keynote and train. It's had an impact on how I write as well.

One of his key teaching moments comes from the concept WIIFM: What's in It for Me. But Jerry sets this idea on its head and instead teaches WIIFY: What's in It for You.

You direct your persuasive words to the reader or listener by saying, "Here's why this product or service is important for you," or "Why should this product matter to you? Here's why," or "Here's why you should take action on this offer now."

Stop making yourself and your company the center of your writing attention. Focus first on the buyers. You'll then better connect and increase your chance to close them.

GIVE THEM A REASON TO BUY <u>NOW</u>

The backbone of this concept comes from the old "impending event" close. In other words, if the buyer doesn't act now, something will change—the price goes up, the product is bought by someone else, the opportunity is lost.

Each time you correspond, you should put some time pressure on the person receiving your e-mail or letter. This urgency could come from quantifying how much money she is losing now. It could come from how much she stands to gain quickly. It could come from shareholder dissatisfaction, lost market share, or personal improvement. Give her a reason not to wait and you strengthen your ability to generate a response to your note.

INCLUDE A CALL TO ACTION

You could end with a distinct call to action, but I'd encourage you to pepper your letter with multiple chances for a buyer to respond.

A great example is built into long-copy, single-page websites. This powerful model for selling online has expert testimonials, reasons to buy, tips, and hints of what you'll receive, and every few paragraphs there's a link to click. "Click this link" to attain all the good things described. "Click this link" and avoid the bad things that are happening now because you don't have what we've got.

Janet Switzer is my favorite secret success story. She's the copywriting genius behind the "Chicken Soup for the Soul" book series and the power marketing genius Jay Abraham. Her bestselling book *Instant Income* is promoted at this one-page website: www.instantincome.com/iibp/. If you print out the "single page" you'll end up with eighteen pages of masterful and persuasive writing.

You can model her structure, which I've done at the following website: www.LeadGenerationGenius.com. Should a single web page serve as an information tool for you, I encourage you to model Switzer's success system for prospecting.

Now, try this exercise: Look at some recent letters you've written, as well as some recent e-mails. Are they prospect-centered (written with more "you" sentences than "we" statements)? Is there some inducement to buy now? Is there a distinct call to action?

One final, fun thought: Look at these next two sentences; they differ by one single, small comma. The meaning changes completely.

"Let's eat Grandma."

"Let's eat, Grandma."

Punctuation saves lives. It saves sales as well.

Pay attention to grammar. Check punctuation and verb tenses. Your impression in print is a permanent reminder of who you are—a pro or an amateur.

Verbal Skills

Another friend, Teri, tells this terrifyingly funny tale about talking too much at the wrong moment. . . .

STOOD UP

My sales manager and I had a full day ahead of us; a three-hour drive to deliver several hourlong presentations, plus the return trip. We began our day anticipating the acquisition of new business.

The town where we were headed held an intriguing opportunity for us. We are accustomed to calling on the Chicago metropolitan area and this was a small town, which was probably not "hit on" by our competitors in our regular territory. Three large companies here could use our services.

We arrived in the town and handled our first two appointments. We excitedly approached our third (and largest) prospect at around 2:00 p.m. We entered the lobby, walked up to the receptionist, and announced our arrival.

The surprised receptionist informed us that our contact had taken the day off! I politely told her that I would call him tomorrow and quickly hustled my sales manager out of the lobby before his "simmering" temper erupted like a volcano. He is very protective of his salespeople's time, and once before he vocalized his displeasure in the lobby of a company after being "stood up."

We got back into the car and started driving out of the parking lot. After a bit of venting, we decided our next step would be to call the prospect's office and leave a voice message saying we were there and will reschedule the appointment. This call was made on my sales manager's cell phone using the speakerphone feature.

After I left the message, my sales manager and I both began to rant again, using some not-so-choice language and graphic detail. This went on for some thirty seconds or so, and then we heard a *Beep!* We realized at that moment, thirty seconds too late, that our entire conversation, with all the acid and anger, had been recorded on the prospect's voice mail!

There was absolutely nothing we could do to undo our stupid blunder. After about two weeks I called the prospect, acting like nothing had happened, to reschedule our appointment.

That was three years ago, and he still won't answer the phone!

Because of the size of the opportunity, every rookie salesperson at Teri's organization will call the company to try for an appointment. To this day, no one has been successful. I guess they'll just have to wait until that buyer with the red-hot ears leaves the company!

When Teri shared her story with me, she begged that the name of her firm and the prospect remain anonymous. I still laugh when I think of how shocking that moment must have been for those two salespeople when that *beep* went off. As my good friend Tony Jeary says, "Life is a series of presentations." (He is the author of a book by the same title.)

Your communication skills send a message in many ways. Do you make the best word choices? Is there energy in your dialogue? Do you physically show strength and confidence and quality in your gestures and smile?

You must be able to present a powerful and persuasive image that shows buyers you are an outstanding communicator who is a true professional in every aspect of your business. Your buyers want to play at the pro level. They want to do business with the most professional partners, to have the most professional image, to buy the most professional solutions. They might not want to pay the pro price, but that's covered in Chapter 12, on objection handling. You should also revisit Chapter 14, which covers first meetings and the importance of the opening strategy for all sales calls, because it gives specifics on language choices to motivate and persuade prospects.

Here, however, in covering verbal skills I also want to mention vocal skills and strength. They are especially important when leaving voice mails and presenting before an audience (by webinar or by PowerPoint). You'll also get a final presentation tip at the end of this section.

VOCAL SKILLS, VOCAL STRENGTH

Let's start with your voice. It is your instrument with which you'll orchestrate great sales conversations. Do you take care of your voice? Today, it's quite popular to hit the health club and stay in shape. Your throat, vocal chords, and tongue need care, too.

Here are seven basic rules in caring for your instrument. They are particularly critical for those of you who do a great deal of phone work.

- Avoid caffeine, chocolate, alcohol, and milk products. The first three dry out the vocal chords; the last increases mucus in the mouth.

- Drink plenty of water, all day long.

- Find your perfect pitch. Hum the song "Happy Birthday." Feel the buzzing, the resonance in the area of your face called your "mask," below the eyes, down to your jaw. That's your perfect pitch. In your perfect pitch you'll sound stronger, more confident, and more comfortable when "playing" your instrument.

- Practice vocal skills. Are you easy to understand? Do you speak too quickly? Take the time to work on enunciating words; it will significantly improve your prospect's ability to hear your message. There's a fun practice chart included here. Work through it regularly and you'll be pleased with improving this area of vocalization.

You can also try saying twisters; you'll be pleased with how well you can improve your vocalization skills. These are included here as well.

▶ Don't yell. It's very hard on your vocal chords. (Confession: I didn't pay much attention to this advice until I had kids. Anyone who has kids, had them, or was one knows what I'm talking about.)

▶ Modulate your voice. Masterful presenters know how to keep listeners' attention by emphasizing words and phrases, by knowing when to increase volume, and by pausing after a key thought is expressed.

▶ Smile! You are speaking to a potential client. The pleasure that sits on the horizon of this presentation, a closed sale, should cause you to smile. When you smile when talking on the phone and when having face-to-face conversations, it'll show up in your voice.

I received fantastic vocal skills training from Susan Berkley of Great Voice http://www.greatvoice.com/. She trains speakers, voice-over artists, actors, and performers. Here are two sets of exercises I still use to warm up and strengthen my voice.

Go through these slowly; they are not tongue twisters. Emphasize each syllable clearly.

Eat each green pea.

Aim straight at the game.

Ed said get ready.

It is in Italy.

I tried my kite.

Oaks grow slowly.

Father was calm as he threw the bomb on the dock.

An awed audience applauded Claude.

Go slow Joe, you're stepping on my toe.

Sauce makes the goose more succulent.

Up the bluff, Bud runs with the cup of love.

Red led men to the heifer that fell in the dell.

Maimed animals may become mean.

It's time to buy a nice limeade for a dime.

Oil soils doilies.

Flip a coin, Roy, you have a choice of oysters or poi.

Sheep shears should be sharp.

At her leisure, she used rouge to camouflage her features.

There's your cue, the curfew is due.

It was the student's duty to deliver the Tuesday newspaper.

He feels keen as he schemes and dreams.

Much of the flood comes under the hutch.

Boots and shoes lose newness soon.

Ruth was rude to the youthful recruit.

Vivid, livid, vivifying, vivid experiences were lived vicariously.

Oddly, the ominous octopus remained calm.

The pod will rot if left on the rock.

Look, you could put your foot on the hood and push.

Nat nailed the new sign on the door of the diner.

Dale's dad died in the stampede for gold.

Thoughtful thinkers think things through.

Engineer Ethelbert wrecked the express at the end of Elm Street.

This next list is tongue twisters. Start slowly; then speed up while trying to make sure your words sound clear and distinct.

Good Blood, Bad Blood, Bad Blood, Good Blood

Around the Rugged Rock the Ragged Rascal Ran

Unique New York

A Real Rare Whale

Double bubble gum bubbles double

Eat fresh fried fish at the fish fry

Sixty-six sick chicks

Tie twine to the tree twigs

Which wily wizard wished wicked wishes for Willy?

Shy Sarah saw six Swiss wristwatches

Used with permission Susan Berkley, The Great Voice Company

I want to leave you with one more tip: I highly recommend you watch late-night talk show hosts if you want a model for voice mastery. First of all, most of them have serious experience as stand-up comedians. They have adopted (and mastered) all of the basic rules I just listed (including and, especially, practicing). Second, like sales pros, they are rewarded directly in proportion to their verbal skills. Finally, they are selling each of their words in order to get their buyer (the audience) to respond with laughter, emotion, or insights that amount to Aha! moments. Watch these performers with a critical eye to discover what they can teach you about improving your vocal skills.

In summary, improve and then master your written and verbal skills and you can be a true sales professional, influencing buyers to buy.

CHAPTER 17

High-Influence Cold Calling

CAN YOU REALLY GET MORE PEOPLE TO CALL YOU BACK?
What you'll learn next is a distinct approach to leaving messages and pitching strangers in person. When my clients put it into play, I would describe their reaction as, well, astonishment.

First, you are going to embody a key *Secret Language of Influence* concept taught throughout this book. That is, you have to distinguish yourself from the competition.

I guarantee you that 98 percent of the salespeople you are up against leave horrible messages. And if they can't land callbacks that turn into appointments, it doesn't matter how good their in-person skills are.

Don't use the traditional pitch. Don't say, "I'm so-and-so from wherever and want to talk about how we can help you . . ." You want to give listeners a choice. Here's a story and an example from which you can model your own approach.

I spent a week with the sales team of a prestigious magazine publisher. Their job was to sell advertising space in their monthly magazine. We crafted the script, as a team, first thing Monday morning. They were then sent to the phones to put it into play. The message went like this:

> Here are the top-three problems we solve for our existing advertisers:
>
> A. We help them stop wasting money on ads that generate feeble responses.
> B. They save money by having access to our award-winning design team that produces unique ads that gain reader attention and response—all at no cost.
> C. They significantly increase response rates by blending print ads to 50,000 readers with our e-mail campaign to 500,000 people who want to know about opportunities like yours.
>
> Which one of these is your biggest concern?

The salespeople started to freak out when prospects actually called back and said, "It's the second one, B, that's my biggest concern." Quite a few buyers even said things like, "It's B, and I'd like to talk about C as well."

The salespeople were also prepared to respond by saying, "Okay, tell me more about that." And everyone was off to the races, moving quickly down the path toward a close.

Deep, deep conversations with the prospect doing most of the talking—that's what a sales call is supposed to look, sound, and feel like. So, get your list together of all the benefits that your customers and prospects gain from your product or service and all the problems your product or service solves. You learned how to compose this list in the chapter on To and Away buyers (see Chapter 2). Select your top three, and start calling.

By the way, think about it. This formula can also serve as your elevator pitch!

There. That was the shortest chapter in the book. Why not go teach this technique to someone today, to anchor your learning. Let me know what happens when you use it, and when your colleagues do, too.

PART TWO

Influencing Yourself

There's an old story about a pro golfer and an amateur (who, in our telling, is also a sales rep). They are on the driving range before a big charity tournament.

The amateur is on his third bucket of balls, nervous about embarrassing himself in front of the pro, his peers, and even the potential clients he might find at the award ceremony.

His pro partner casually walks up to the practice tee with a driver over his shoulder. He reaches into a pocket, pulls out five balls, and drops them on the mat. He lines up the first ball, hits it, and ninety seconds later has finished smacking the other four. He turns to head back to the clubhouse.

The sales rep is stunned. "Excuse me, but is that it? Is that your whole warm-up routine?"

The pro smiles and says, "If you didn't bring it with you, you're not going to find it here."

If you didn't bring it with you, you're not going to find it here.

What message does that statement send to you about getting ready to sell?

The chapters in Part 2 reveal the best practices of business pros who are so mentally healthy, so mentally tough, that they bring it to the selling table every single day. They let nothing deter them from giving a world-class sales performance and having a world-class career.

In other words, they influence themselves so well that they can handle anything in their selling life, as well as in their personal life.

Get ready for some great insights into persuading yourself.

CHAPTER 18

Seven Keys to Influencing Your Brain

YOUR BRAIN IS YOU. In this chapter, we'll look at what I call the seven keys to influencing your brain. They are:

1. Rejection

2. Resilience

3. Goals

4. Priorities

5. Balance

6. Attitude

7. Self-talk

As you read on, try to think of times in your selling career or your personal life when your brain (that is, you!) was influenced by each of them.

Rejection

Rejection is a very close cousin to resilience. Since easily 90 percent of our selling interactions are negative (we don't get called back, our e-mails are ignored, tough-as-nails gatekeepers won't show us the way in, we don't win the account), it amazes me how individuals in our profession are so influenced by something as normal as rejection.

And we have a tricky relationship with rejection's close relative: *resilience*. At one point we need to push forward, keep knocking, calling, e-mailing. At another point we need to give up and move on.

If you let rejection influence you too strongly, you'll bail out of our profession. If you can influence your brain to be resilient, but smart, you'll toughen up and stick around for a long, profitable career.

Let's look at both rejection and resilience. We'll adopt some smart ways to manage both as we navigate our way through the sights and sounds of our selling lives.

I was invited into a meeting with a team that headed up global sales training with one of the largest sales forces in the world. It was a network marketing organization. Because the salespeople were typical consumers, virtually none of them had any selling experience. Of those with sales experience, the percentage with actual training was tiny. I asked the senior executive to tell me what new salespeople are told to do, once they commit to the company.

"They're told that their first contacts—[much like the people a new insurance sales rep contacts]—are friends, family, and neighbors." And he added, "It's tough, but get a couple of these people to buy, and you're on your way."

Oh, a vital statistic here. He mentioned that 95 percent of new recruits bust out—they fail.

I decided to respond to the executive with a story.

Picture this: You're the new rep. You flag down Bill, your neighbor, in his driveway before work one day. This is awkward for a dozen different reasons: Your newness means you have no idea what's going to happen, how he will respond, what kind of objections you'll hear.

You pitch a meeting, an opportunity, a product. It doesn't matter which, because Bill squints at you with a confused look that says, "Are you kidding me?" Then he actually says, "Uh, no thanks. See ya later." He darts into his car and pulls away.

You slink back to the house, embarrassed. No, that's not a strong enough word. You're humiliated, but hopeful.

The next day you see Bill leaving for work and offer a feeble wave. He nods his head and launches himself quickly into the car.

After work you don't even walk near the window that looks on his house. In fact, you decide to close the shades so that you two don't accidently even glance at one another.

Your coach who signed you up has some tips and encouraging words. But you then call a family member who chuckles and says "No thanks" to this meeting you desperately want people to attend.

Eventually someone says *yes*; perhaps even a few people do. But nobody buys. Or maybe one or two will, but, man, this selling stuff is hard!

Two or three weeks later you boldly walk up to the neighbor. "Hey, Bill! Real quick, I'm not doing that network marketing thing anymore. I don't have enough time, it wasn't as much money as I thought, and the organization isn't what I believed, but the products are great and we still use them. Anyway, when did you want to get out like we talked about last month and see that new sports bar across town?"

What you're really saying to Bill is that you want to move beyond the awkwardness from the rejection you received when you put him in a bad place a month ago. You want to be friends and neighbors again.

I paused after telling this story and stared at the executive. Then I offered my analysis, saying: "Maybe what's really happened is that your newbies have failed in the business because they'd rather maintain relationships than make more money. Or rejection is so hard on them that they avoid it by drifting away from your business opportunity, in spite of the evidence that plenty of people are successful and make good money doing it. What if that crazy, large percentage of people fail, perhaps on purpose, simply because they are unprepared for rejection—because they have no strategy, no self-talk to move past it? What if they'd rather be in relationships with others than in business with you?"

Awkward (but to me, very interesting) silence descended upon the room. The executive was agape.

Here's a key concept: If you don't prepare sales reps for rejection and failure, those negative experiences can color the salesperson's view of selling so darkly, they might lead to the rep rejecting sales as a career altogether.

It's been my experience that the "hump" in selling for rookies is six months. Get your new reps over the hump with enough success to generate a desire for more of it and you're building a potential champion in the field or on the phone.

But how do you prepare sales reps, regardless of experience, to deal with the dark side of the selling world—rejection?

For twenty or more years, many managers and trainers have taught a simple phrase to sales pros about what to do when rejection occurs. It's this: "Yes, no, next."

Got the sale? Then you've got the "Yes." Good. Move on. "Next!"

Got a "No"? Good. Move on. "Next!"

Yes, no, next.

If that is a bit simplistic, or if you have reps who are longer-winded (even when talking to themselves!), teach them a phrase they're most comfortable with that points to a positive future. Examples:

"I'm getting the next one."

"That's fine. I'm great at what I do. One miss doesn't mark me."

You get the idea. Look up at life, not down. It's potent self-talk (more on this topic later in the chapter) for your reps to use.

That's how to manage resistance. It's nothing complex; it's almost too simple to work.

When will you start to say and believe, "Yes, no, next"?

Resilience

Now, how about rejection's cousin, resilience? Great sales pros can stay positive and push through anything. That's a rough definition of "resilience." And no surprise: It's a critical characteristic for selling pros. What are some types of thinking and behavior that are evident in resilient people?

Factors That Identify Resilient People

- They move on quickly. ("Yes, no, next" is a good start.)
- They are flexible (smart) enough to change when necessary.
- They know what their beliefs are and stand by them.
- They have a strong sense of right and wrong.
- They are not swayed by the crowd.
- They remain optimistic.
- They focus on completion of their goals and on success—not perfection.
- They are open to criticism, but not necessarily swayed by it. Nor are they hurt by it.
- They rely on the belief in their body of work as assurance, not the most recent success or failure.

Consider that your checklist on resilience. Which of the items on the list will you check off as done? If you have to print it out and keep it handy, that's not a bad idea. Put a page in your car, in the office, and how about at home, too? As I said from the beginning, organic influence strategies work anywhere. Share this information with a spouse, a kid, a close friend.

Resilience persuades you to keep focused on your goals, which we'll cover next.

Goals

Here's a nice technique I used when I was training a publishing company's sales team. It is useful for helping sales reps own their successful behaviors.

You work backward from the reps' desired commissions to identify which daily activities are essential to attaining their goals.

When salespeople record data on number of calls, appointments or meetings set, closing ratio, and size of sale, they are able to see, in their own handwriting, what kind of commitment they need to make in order to make the kind of money they want. They do their own calculations, rather than having some gross dollar figure handed to them.

I usually say during the training, "If anyone has a problem with the calculations, raise your hand." On one occasion, the person who raised her hand was a very good customer service rep that someone decided to convert to a sales rep. Her name was Catherine. I looked over her shoulder and was shocked to see that her base activity was to make 2.5 phone calls a day! Two and a half phone calls over the course of eight hours.

"Catherine," I whispered, "how much money in commissions are you hoping to make this year?"

She whispered back, "$5,000."

Huh? Turns out, as a sales rep, she now had a base of $25,000 selling. If she made five grand in commissions, that'd be a nice raise for a customer service rep.

Okay, so moving Catherine to a sales role was a mistake. And here's the real issue you want to address with your salespeople: How good are your goals?

Goal setting is a tricky place, from the training perspective. You've hired upbeat, optimistic people and they probably have higher expectations than they'll attain. But that's a good thing. It is lower expectations that are bad.

When you have a simple formula that reps can individually work through, they own the details of their goals. That bears repeating a third time. You'll read exactly how to influence your behaviors using this method in Chapter 21, "Know Your Numbers," where I'll give an extended example.

For now, let's look at that old tried-and-true acronym for goal setting: SMART. As you know, SMART stands for specific, measurable, attainable, realistic, and timely. Craft those concepts into a single phrase like, "By December 31, 20xx, I will earn $75,000 in commissions above my base salary in order to have enough money to buy that new Lexus hybrid SUV."

This brings us to the other part of goal setting. That is, casting a vision for attaining something beyond work. You earn money to spend on people and places and things. In sales, we generate discretionary funds for ourselves, all day long. So what will you do to fulfill your dreams with the money you acquire?

The word *vision* denotes something you see, albeit in the future. This is why your SMART goals are never complete until you can picture them.

Not long ago I trained a sales team that had no visual imagery in the office to denote the team's potential sales, closed business, goals, or anything else. It was a huge effort to create a chart that always served to let them know where they were in the company's eyes. While the sales reps take charge of caring for their personal goals (the vacation, the vehicle, the toy of choice), the firm should cast a vision, month by month, throughout the year, so reinforcement comes constantly. When everyone understands company and individual goals, you create accountability and some competitiveness that is healthy and uplifting.

When will you influence your goals by creating a visual reminder of those aims? Where will that reminder go? Who will you share it with, in order to hold your feet to the fire in attaining the goal?

Let's look next at priorities, get some tricks on identifying and managing them, and recognize how they are the key to influencing behaviors that lead us to our goals.

Priorities

Picture this: You are at SeaWorld and a whale trainer says she needs three volunteers to help feed Shamu. Three thousand hands fly toward heaven, accompanied by screams of joy, anticipation, and hope. "Pick me! Me first!"

As one guest is selected, the other 2,999 become even more frantic for your attention. After all, their chances have just been reduced by 33 percent. When the second volunteer is chosen, only one spot is left. The noise could deafen a submerged whale. You get the idea. Those waving hands and shouting voices are symbolic of every personal and professional activity rioting for your attention. The issues are:

▸ Why should we prioritize?

▸ What will we prioritize?

▸ How will we prioritize?

WHY DO WE PRIORITIZE?

If we don't rank the value of our activities, we function by default. Imagine how dangerous it would be to make decisions this way. To operate our lives, every day, by reacting to the loudest voice behind the hand raised highest. So who runs your selling life? Whatever you choose to react to. Yet it is not necessarily in your best interests to make responding to pressure the basis of your business decisions!

Prioritizing has clear benefits to the sales professional. Setting priorities:

- Eliminates procrastination

- Gives great focus during the workday

- Helps you attend to your strengths

- Teaches delegation of low-level tasks

- Keeps income-related activities at the top of the list

What other reasons can you think of that make prioritizing a priority?

WHAT DO WE PRIORITIZE?

For sales professionals, priorities should focus on the acquisition of money; how much time and energy their sales activities take (don't underestimate energy!); how those activities help attain goals (both personal and corporate); whether to attend to interruptions; and perhaps most important, the development of our time management skills. Every task should have a deadline, even if you have to create one yourself to see it to completion.

Setting priorities simply mirrors goal-setting concepts. Sales pros who prioritize are less likely to procrastinate. They focus on income-producing activities first.

Here's the toughest part of what we prioritize. Absolutely decide that when you have access to buyers, you must be attempting to gain access and get that initial conversation or appointment. That means no paperwork or administrative activities; you must think of nothing but getting the sales funnel filled and business closed.

If you have too many things to do that keep you from focusing this way, then you need to figure out how to do them outside buying hours. You may have to work a bit earlier or later, or else automate some processes and/or hire a sales assistant. (Do the numbers and figure out how that person's salary trades off in increased sales.)

HOW DO WE PRIORITIZE?

You won't like my advice here. There's a list, then an idea. You'll wonder, "Can I run my business that way?" Yes, you can.

First, you are looking at your day's work and trying to figure out what's first, what's most important, what's going to make you the most money (and fastest). How do you teach reps to prioritize their workload?

There are many ways to identify how to prioritize activities. Not all of the traditional categories apply to sales professionals. Those listed here include descriptions as well as some useful cautions.

Urgency or Due Date. This is the most obvious way to prioritize because deadlines cry for attention. Be cautious of the value here. Does completion lead to revenue? If not, can the deadline be extended? Can it be delegated to others?

Volume or Weight of the Work. Heavy loads can be chunked into small pieces daily to chip away at the large task. Again, don't let this workload function as a mountain summit whose sheer size cries for your attention. What can be delegated? Can you climb the mountain of tasks slower? How about later?

Persistent Pressure. Don't be shamed into attending to other people's needs. Keep your focus, learn to manage those relationships, and let people know that you'd love to help (if true), but your concerns take precedent.

Ease. Do you prefer to knock off some simple tasks and feel better for having eliminated "to-do" list items? Here's a hint: If you have energy problems during the day, work through the easy activities at this time (there's more advice on managing energy levels in Chapter 20).

Difficulty. Do you prefer to remove hard tasks in order to feel relief at knowing they are behind you?

Problem Popping Up. Sometimes some things cry suddenly for immediate attention. Because we rely so much on e-mail and texting, people either expect an immediate response or feel they have to attend immediately to everything. Digital or not (e-mail, text, people, or phones), intrusions happen. Can you ignore it? Can you delay responding? Just because it's a problem doesn't mean it should derail the plans and priorities of your day.

Passion. Is it just more fun to work on something you love to do? Just be aware that this tendency can serve as a distraction from more important issues.

A Recommended "How to Prioritize" Strategy

- Block out parts of your day and stick to them religiously, as if you believe there's a god of sales who smiles on this behavior.

- As a sales professional you want to train your buyers to respect that you are busy (which means successful) and not just sitting around waiting for the phone to ring.

- When you leave a voice mail, you want to tell the person that you are available only from the time you choose later in the day (e.g., from 4:00 to 4:30 p.m.). Otherwise you are serving clients. The sample structure here is just that, a suggestion:

Yesterday 4:30–5:00 p.m.	Plan tomorrow's calls and workload
8:00–10:00 a.m.	Make 40–60 phone calls, outgoing only!
10:00–10:10 a.m.	Break
10:10–11:45 a.m.	Respond to messages/return phone calls
11:45 a.m.–12:45 p.m.	Lunch
12:45–3:00 p.m.	Face-to-face calls
3:00–4:00 p.m.	Outgoing calls
4:00–4:30 p.m.	Respond to messages/return phone calls
4:30–5:00 p.m.	Plan tomorrow's calls and workload

Notice that you end each day by planning the next day in detail. This is a huge time-saver. You walk into work and start to work. No buzzing about, figuring out whom to call, what to do. Your coworkers will notice your strange (but productive) behavior and begin to leave you alone as they respect and eventually envy your abundant output.

The concept is important, not the example. I promise you, if you settle into a similar routine of your own design, you will be productive like you've never been.

Remember, when selling on the phone our job is to interrupt the prospect, not the other way around. There's a principle in persuasion called "scarcity." This means things or people that are harder to access are more desirable.

You want to creatively build your system, and then follow it. There will be exceptions and you'll prioritize those, and then move on. That's how you prioritize your activities in a concrete way.

Now, what will your daily work flow look like?

Balance

John is a good friend of mine. We're both competitive athletes who had the good fortune (and hard-work ethic) to enjoy sports careers beyond college. Our kids are the same age and work out together. John is a money manager—one of the most stressful jobs you can find.

One afternoon he called me after the stock market closed to say a client was angry because John lost the man $200,000. Now this investor is worth hundreds of millions of dollars. And the mistake was actually that the client ignored a call from John and didn't respond to a request to approve a stock play until after a dip in the market.

But who cares about fault? The client, my friend's paycheck, was irate.

I asked John how he handled the anxiety related to this type of work. He said, "Dan, do you know that the average person who does what I do doesn't make it to age 58?"

And I said, "That's your answer? You handle it by dying at age 57? You mean people make a conscious decision to die early, but before that they enjoy extraordinarily high earnings?"

Death. There's the ultimate sacrifice for job-related stress. This issue is exactly why many major corporations (led by the insurance industry, no less) are putting into place mandatory vacation policies for executives. Most of this massive emotional and physical strain comes from our inability to disconnect our personal and professional lives.

This section fits into another discussion, in Chapter 20, on the sales professional's mental health, because everyone on your selling team needs to make a conscious decision to create separation and balance from work. This separation doesn't only happen with vacation. The Human Performance Institute teaches business professionals to disconnect regularly. You should escape mentally and physically during each month, each week, even during the workday. The energy gained is significant. (Chapter 20 has a fascinating story on how the basis for this teaching comes from research into world-class tennis players.)

For now, let's look at a solution offered by the prestigious Mayo Clinic. As long as you are working, juggling the demands of career and personal life is probably going to be an ongoing challenge. Use these seven ideas to help you find the work-life balance that's best for you:

▶ *Track your time.* Track everything you do for one week, including work-related and personal activities. Decide what's necessary and what satisfies you the most. Cut or delegate activities you don't enjoy or can't handle—or share your concerns and possible solutions with your employer or others.

▶ *Take advantage of your options.* Ask your employer about flex hours, a compressed workweek, job sharing, telecommuting, or other scheduling flexibility. The more control you have over your hours, the less stressed you are likely to be.

▶ *Learn to say* no. Whether it's a coworker asking you to spearhead an extra project or your child's teacher asking you to direct the class play, remember that it's okay to respectfully say *no.* When you quit doing the things you do only out of guilt or a false sense of obligation, you'll make more room in your life for the activities that are meaningful to you and bring you joy.

▶ *Leave work at work.* With the technology to connect to anyone at any time from virtually anywhere, there may be no boundary between work and home—unless you create it. Make a conscious decision to separate work time from personal time. When you are with your family, for instance, turn off your cell phone and put away your laptop computer.

▶ *Manage your time.* Organize household tasks efficiently, such as running errands in batches or doing a load of laundry every day, rather than saving it all for your day off. Put family events on a weekly family calendar and keep a daily to-do list. Do what needs to be done and let the rest go. Limit time-consuming misunderstandings by communicating clearly and listening carefully. Take notes if necessary.

▶ *Bolster your support system.* At work, join forces with coworkers who can cover for you—and vice versa—when family conflicts arise. At home, enlist trusted friends and loved ones to pitch in with child care or household responsibilities when you need to work overtime or travel.

▶ *Nurture yourself.* Eat healthy foods, include physical activity in your daily routine, and get enough sleep. Set aside time each day for an activity that you enjoy, such as practicing yoga or reading. Better yet, discover activities you can do with your partner, family, or friends—such as hiking, dancing, or taking cooking classes.[11]

The Mayo Clinic also suggests you should seek professional help when your ability to manage these issues becomes too much for you and you feel a loss of control over them.

Stop here and carefully consider those seven Mayo Clinic bullets. Make a checklist and mark the things you do well. Increase your sensitivity to work-life balance. The benefits are sitting right in front of you. The problems that come with a lack of balance can wreck families. Remember what we're in the game for—to enjoy our earnings with people we love.

Attitude

Here you'll discover my favorite technique to influence attitude.

A sales rep's attitude forms the foundation of her interaction with the world. It colors how she views her prospects, how she deals with coworkers, and how she dialogues with family and friends to start and end each day.

An organization can be energized by great attitudes. In contrast, one sour attitude can spoil a meeting or a day. One way I've trained reps to start their day optimistically is to tell them: *Don't listen to radio on your way to work.*

Fill your mind with upbeat healthy things, not negative news. Listen instead to music you love, or to a great audio recording of a favorite book or selling ideas. But use that time to prepare for the day in a healthy, optimistic way.

Bad thoughts can infect you with feelings that are difficult to shake. I even used to send reps home in extreme cases if they had an experience so bad that they became distraught: "No hard feelings, Megan, go have some fun and forget about some lousy buyer who didn't come through. Have a great afternoon; we'll see you tomorrow when we start fresh."

You could argue this is foolish and doesn't help her work through rejection, but I found that once in a while it did more good for the team as well as the individual.

Today, I preempt those problems with a specific approach to influence. One of the finest ways to help your sales pros adopt a healthy attitude is to have them focus on gratitude. Read this next example of fascinating research and see how it forms the basis for some interesting learning moments.

POORLY PAID INSECTS

An entomologist at Cornell University has worked out that the annual value of insect services in the United States is around $57 billion. Insect services include crop pollination and land cleaning.[12]

Outside the knowledge of more than 300 million Americans, insects are doing work for us, and not getting paid. And they are doing it without our permission. Aside from the fact that scientists at an Ivy League school probably got paid a few hundred thousand of our tax dollars to do this speculative research, there's a lesson here for salespeople, and it's related to the theme of being grateful for what we have.

Here's the lesson, in a question: Who is helping in the background?

Go beyond the obvious. It's not about the sales assistant or marketing team or anyone you are closely aligned with in your selling day. Let's make it about the other people with whom you have limited contact but who support you nonetheless. Internally, it might be accounting/finance and HR people. Externally, it might be suppliers or the actual manufacturers of the products you sell.

Here's an exercise I do in training. I suggest that you try it, too: Sit down with your team in your next meeting, or with your networking group, or by yourself, if you are selling solo. Identify who is in the background contributing to your success.

Then thank them.

Send a note, flowers, goodies to eat, something that says, "You're important to me and I want to acknowledge you." Watch the energy soar around you. Observe the difference it makes when attitude improves, even for just a day. That should give you something to anchor on, to recognize how valuable an upbeat attitude can be within an organization.

But how do you keep attitudes elevated each day on an ongoing basis?

One of my favorite training experiences was a day of call coaching with World Vision (www.worldvision.org). This fund-raising organization is recognized as one of the finest charities in the world, with the vast majority of its donations going directly to service the needs of underresourced people around the planet. Per their website: "We continually strive to keep our overhead rate low. In 2010, 85 percent of our total operating expenses were used for programs that benefit children, families, and communities in need."

Because World Vision keeps costs so low, many of its phone callers are students, graduates fresh out of school, and part-time workers. Youth and inexperience can seriously affect attitudes. Imagine making forty to sixty phone calls a day and getting rejected constantly—even when calling existing donors. Add into the mix the fact that a tough economy is especially hard on both fund-raisers and donors. I recognized these conditions and created an exercise to build up World Vision fund-raisers' attitude in their training day.

Self-Talk

I'm coaching the base paths on my son's little league team. We have runners on first and third when our batter hits the ball to the pitcher.

The boy on the base in front of me breaks for home plate and I yell, "Stop, come back!"

The pitcher turns and stares. There's this big, collective "Oohhh!" from the crowd as parents realize, just as my runner realizes, that . . .

He's running home from first base!

I have no idea how the nerve synapses misfired in little Matt's mind, but I do know this—he is heading in the wrong direction and disastrous consequences are about to result. The boy is tagged out sliding into home and walks back to the dugout, fighting back tears.

I wave off his dad, who is walking over from the stands, immediately sit down next to Matt, and ask him what he said to himself when that happened. This, by the way, is what I recommend people do with anyone they care about. Kids, loved ones, friends—ask them what they say, in their head, when things go poorly. Managing this kind of situation is huge for a child's self-esteem. You want to catch it early, with both kids and sales reps.

Matt says, "I really suck at baseball. I can't do anything right." This thinking is pure poison for a kid and sets him up for future failure.

My response (and you'll soon see how it fits the model for dealing with self-talk) is this: "Matt, you just hit a single to get on base, right? You're one of the team's best fielders. You're fast and everyone loves you as a teammate. Let's look at your experience with baseball in a different way. Can you do that?"

Matt says, "Uh, I did get a hit and I scored twice last game. And Mom and Dad said I was so good last time, they treated me to three scoops of ice cream afterward. I guess sometimes I'm good at this game."

"Great!" I reply. "Whenever you come to bat or run the bases or field a ball, I want you to say to yourself—I point to my head— 'I'm great at this game.' You keep saying that, instead of negative things. Can you do that? Let me hear it now."

"I'm great at this game."

"Really, Matt. I believe it. Do you?" He's nodding by now, but I say, "Tell me again."

"I'm great at this game."

Strong self-talk can set anyone on a path of encouragement, hope, and positive beliefs about his abilities. My fascination with the power of self-talk is off the charts. It's just not taught in sales training. So one time I decided to run a surprise quiz with a client's sales team.

I began like this: "On a piece of paper write down, right now, what you say in your head immediately when you lose a sale or when something you hoped/expected to have happen does not. Be honest, use your exact words."

The sheets I collected were very entertaining reading. A great deal of words began with the letter *F*.

I then dug a bit deeper. I addressed the group, saying, "Here's what Joe said. Well, I can't read all of it, but here it is, with all my edits." Then I read his comments about lost sales and afterward said, "So, Joe, tell me more about your response." I received some fascinating feedback, things like, "I hate when people say *no*," and "Either these prospects are stupid or I can't communicate well enough to persuade them to switch companies."

I like to tell sales pros, athletes, and kids that you should focus on things you can control, not what you cannot. And we *can* increase our communication skills.

But what does the research show that we do about negative self-talk?

Martin Seligman, the father of positive psychology, has focused on differences in success and performance of optimists vs. pessimists. His groundbreaking works *Learned Optimism* and, later, *Authentic Happiness* teach us that negative thought patterns can limit our present and future potential in both professional and personal relationships. That's why I start my training module on positive self-talk (after a story, of course) by saying, "Today we'll learn to undo what Seligman refers to as 'catastrophic thoughts.' Someone define that term, please." ·

I want you to discover how to work the psychological magic of positive self-talk on your kids, your sales reps, and others. In fact, it's the same technique I use when coaching kids in sports. Let's say one of my players (but not my son) strikes out. I immediately sit him down and ask what he said in his head when he was called out. Fixing self-esteem requires going through a process where we learn to *argue with ourselves*. This process also makes for memorable and potentially long-lasting learning.

NOTES

1. Mayo Clinic staff, "Work-Life Balance: Tips to Reclaim Control," http://www.mayoclinic.com/health/work-life-balance/WL00056/NSECTION GROUP=2.

2. NewScientist.com, citing the April 2006 issue of the journal *Bioscience*; for original, see John E. Losey and Mace Vaughan, "The Economic Value of Ecological Services Provided by Insects," *Bioscience* 56, No. 4 (April 2006), pp. 311–323.

CHAPTER 19

Heart and Head Check: Self-Test

FROM THE BIG PICTURE, DOWN . . . In this chapter, you will make a funnel for your business, from big picture issues (e.g., economy, your industry) down to details (e.g., your job, yourself). On a piece of paper, create *positive responses* to your feelings about each of the items listed here. Sample answers follow; for purposes of illustration, I'm using the example of someone who works in fund-raising.

The Economy
Things are hard now, but people really do have more money than they need. If someone gives up a case of Coke a month, it can help.

Fund-Raising Industry
The tough economy is hard on our industry. But fund-raisers do good work, helping people who have much less than us.

Your Company, World Vision

I work for one of the most prestigious, respected, and ethical organizations on the planet and am proud of it!

Donors' Perception About World Vision

They trust that ten cents on every dollar goes to running the organization while ninety cents helps the people they see on our website and in TV commercials.

Your Office

My work environment is bright and easy to work in, with fun employees and the newest computers and phones.

Your Boss

Larry is easy to work with and really cares about me personally, as well as my work role.

Your Job

I get to interact with interesting people from all over the country and from all walks of life. It's a cool reflection of God's diverse creation, all experienced on the phone.

Yourself

I landed a job here! It's a lot of work and fun, too. Every day I try to contribute a little more than the day before.

▶ ▶ ▶

Notice how healthy responses found light at the end of every tunnel. For example, on the industry level, the response was about people being served by fund-raising organizations, rather than the tight wallets of today's donors.

Of course, your checklist will be slightly different from the example provided. It will refer specifically to your industry (financial services, information technology, manufacturing, retail, etc.), your company (by name), and the perceptions of your "buyers" (rather than donors).

Print out the positive responses you are able to create by taking this exercise. Then post them on your desk and on the walls of your office, and see how uplifting this checklist is for anyone walking into the work area. You just branded healthy attitude inside the company.

Reps on the road? They can create and take their list with them and peek at it as often as needed.

Here's something else to try with this exercise. E-mail a blank version of the document to each of your sales reps; then have them run this exercise at home (e.g., rewriting the list for their marriage, for kids, for family, or anyone they connect with) or teach it to other salespeople or entrepreneurs or association and networking colleagues. Remember, the best learners become teachers as soon as they come across new knowledge.

Change attitude by focusing on gratitude. And change it forever by giving people printed evidence of all the good they encounter and offer each day.

The chart you create serves as a great visual aid. You can influence your attitude by taking the high road with plenty of healthy gratitude.

I like the following quote, because it embodies how deeply affected we are by the act of arguing, even when that includes arguing with ourselves.

> *Did you ever argue in a relationship so much, that's how you remember where you were—"Didn't we argue here once?"*
>
> —Comedian Todd Glass

Let's look at why and how I encourage pleasant self-talk.

Three Steps to Healthy and Potent Self-Talk

1. *Recognize an idea that resounds in your head with disgust or despair.* For example: "I hate when prospects say *no*. Either this guy is stupid to miss how well I can help him, or I can't communicate well enough to persuade him to switch."

2. *Check your perceptions against real evidence or facts.* "I guess, in reality, this man runs a very successful company, so he can't

really be stupid. And I communicate great at the office, at home, and with the excellent clients I already have."

3. *Rewrite your self-talk.* "This sale wasn't going to happen when I didn't discover something important because I should have asked some good questions. That's my weak area in selling. I'm good at managing clients and I sell fairly well. I could be better 'cause I know what to work on." You need to show accurate, logical facts that affect your ability to sell, or at least give you a healthy perspective on reality. By arguing this way, you separate beliefs from facts and can mentally rewrite them based on logic and evidence.

Use positive language: **do vs. don't.**

The Power of Positive Self-Talk

Let your sales team members, each and every one of them, find their own voice. Let them determine positive language to use, in their head, when they encounter any situation—both good and bad—in their selling life. They'll move quickly past success and failure, whether large or small, and keep working on the next prospect, the next proposal, the next win.

You will love that your healthy self-talk will eventually bleed into your real conversations during the day. You'll be a more optimistic person in the work environment and, more important, at home. And I can't think of a better way to influence anyone than to be the person whom others love to hang around with.

CHAPTER 20

Influence Your Body

MEETING PLANNING MISERY . . . I love this story. A sales rep named Joel shared it during my "confession session" at a keynote I did at an International Special Events Society (ISES) program in Chicago.

Joel Jumps on a Prospect Early in the Day

As an ISES member, Joel's company provides event-planning services for national sales conferences and yearly corporate celebrations. He had an office at home in Denver. Thanks to the time zone difference, he was always working. He would call East Coast prospects and clients before he went to work. He would do paperwork after he got home.

He was a hermit, a recluse—none of his friends had seen him in six months.

One evening he was assaulted by phone calls from everyone he knew. What was wrong with him? Had he given up on bars and all the good stuff that came with them—music, beer, women?

So, with the threat of total abandonment by his buddies, Joel took a cab to the club. He made up for six months of alcohol abstinence in one night. Here's his first-person account of what happened next:

It's 3:00 a.m. Bleary-eyed and blitzed, I stagger home. Having programmed myself to do so, I wander right into my office there.

I grab my phone and call my biggest prospect—a company that spent over a quarter-million dollars on its yearly sales conference.

Sputtering and slobbering into the mouthpiece, I pitched him.

"Oh, please, you've got to buy from me. You're the biggest company I've ever called on. I can do a great job, I swear. Besides, my commission on this project would be beyond belief. Please use me for your event planning. We're the best. You've got to give me a chance."

I passed out on my desk. The screeching dial tone from the disconnected phone didn't even wake me up. There was only one phone call the next day. I missed it because I was out cold and I didn't get to the office.

It was the guy I had reached out to, in my sorry state. "Uh, Joel, I believe it was you that called my office at three in the morning. Please don't ever call me or our company again."

For all the big sales meetings I've keynoted, trained at, and attended over the years, I had never thought about the reps who are selling event management services to coordinate hotel bookings and food services. I've begun to collect some wild tales from these planning pros.

But this story embodies the value of rest, recovery, and energy in a salesperson's life.

Jim Loehr and Jack Groppel had done extensive research on the concept of personal energy at the Human Performance Institute (HPI) in Orlando, Florida. These two men started by training world-class tennis players. Over the years, their work evolved into teaching best practices that help business professionals attain world-class skills by managing energy.

Their foundational belief is that managing energy could be more critical to success than managing time. Energy comes from taking breaks during the business day, the week, the month, and the year. This concept covers how well you mentally and physically leave your work behind or "disconnect." For some great details on this concept, I highly recommend Loehr's book *The Power of Full Engagement,* and Groppel's book *The Corporate Athlete.*

Some of their tips include:

- Creating positive rituals to manage your daily work efforts (e.g., building breaks into the workday to help you rest and recover from those efforts) and the techniques for building those rituals

- Understanding life balance that covers physical conditioning as well as emotional, mental, and spiritual wellness

- Eating properly, moving around and getting fresh air, even playing (mentally and physically) to disconnect so that you can rest and recover from work

- Recognizing barriers to managing energy, in order to plan for overcoming them

- Creating accountability to employ the new learning and accompanying behaviors

All of their advice amounts to being fully engaged in your work, because you don't burn out while seeking success.

I took the Corporate Athlete training and recognized that the "putting the pedal to the metal" mindset is good as long as you get off the gas and out of the car a few times a day. I disconnect during my day by getting out of my office and into the sun, or by watching some short videos or reading humor books (I don't read business writing that recycles my brain right back to what I'm supposed to be leaving behind). You can take a free Full Engagement Profile in five minutes at the HPI website (www.hpinstitute.com/assessment-tools).

So gather energy through the workday—eat right, move around, get that fresh air (even in winter), disconnect from your work, and play. What do you dwell on? Take your mind to a place other than work.

You can also manage energy by going to bed earlier every night. Then recover and gain energy by getting up earlier every day. Do the numbers. Even at thirty extra minutes multiplied by 250 days a year, you gain more than three extra weeks of work. That's 17 percent more work, or 17 percent more commission a year. What if, instead, you woke up an hour earlier and increased earnings by a third?

Let's also focus for a bit on food. But first a warning: You're about to read some foundational practices from the natural health community. Some of my comments might run counter to what traditional medicine would have you believe. You need to get the advice of your doctor before you attempt anything that I describe as my practice. Okay? I'm not a physician.

When I've managed sales teams, and in my coaching practice, I talk about how nutrition can affect performance. Eating healthy, getting exercise, and getting rest is not just good advice from Mom. Here are a few rules that I plan to expand upon in a future book, or in my next keynote, if you have a sales event and want to open it with humor and smart ideas for your team.

1. The *worst* foods in the world are french fries and doughnuts. Anytime you eat something that is fried through and through, your body cannot digest it. Now, if you could find a way to get your internal temperature up to 300+ degrees and liquefy the oil that has crystallized in the food, you'd be fine. But you can't. So don't eat them, ever.

2. You eat for fuel first, not for fun. Be smart about what you put into your body and you'll live longer and healthier. You know it's true, so stop rationalizing about deserving and rewarding and all that crap. When you are in fantastic shape, reward yourself with something fun (i.e., bad) once a week, but not once a day, and certainly not throughout the day.

3. Exercise at least three times a week, but five would be better. No excuses! You can exercise in front of the TV (though that could make you simultaneously stronger and stupider).

4. Rest and recovery are critical for your body's health. Think of your body as a wavy line that's speeding up, working hard, slowing down, cooling off. You can go hard as long as you rest well and often. Hey, interesting coincidence: This up-and-down pattern is like the wavy line on a heart machine. It indicates health. And a flat line? Well, that indicates death.

5. Often, disease centers on your flawed digestive process. Food that doesn't get used in the body sits there and not only turns into fat, but sticks in your intestines and ferments, leaching toxins into your body. So, keeping in mind my earlier warning that I am not a doctor and you should check with yours first, here comes my Clean Up Your Act! advice. . . .

Go do a good intestinal cleanse. It's the *first* thing anyone should do who wants to get truly healthy. The program I've encouraged tons of people to do (friends as well as business relationships) is a two-week program. You don't have to fast. The first week you simply take some herbal pills with dinner. That's easy enough, right? The second week you take some powder in water, five to six times a day. This powder sticks to the bad stuff in your intestines and eventually pries it off the walls of your intestines and it leaves by, well, you get the picture—your normal process of elimination. Sounds a bit awful, but you'd rather have that junk in your toilet than in your body.

At the risk of straying into "too much information" territory, I'll share a story with you about getting into great health: I do an intestinal cleanse once a year, in January. I'm in what doctors call "outstanding shape." I still compete internationally in basketball on the U.S. World Masters' team; I play the sport three times weekly and lift weights three times a week as well. Nobody who knows me would think I could do anything more with my physical condition or appearance. All this means I have energy to work hard and long hours, when I need to. And my health and competitive instincts parallel my attitude in sales—*I hate losing more than I like winning.*

How about it, sales pros? Will you clean up your act? Will you stop playing with your health and energy. Discover how well you will sell when you are physically able to work both longer and stronger!

CHAPTER 21

Know Your Numbers

UNUSED FREQUENT FLYER MILES AND SELLING . . .
Economist magazine once reported that the value of unused frequent flyer miles in global circulation exceeded the total amount of U.S. dollars in worldwide circulation. The calculation was based on 14 trillion miles at two cents each, giving a total value of U.S. $700 billion.[1]

What do you collect and measure in your sales life? Is your currency phone calls? Prospects? Closed deals? Time spent in the office? Time spent at home?

Isn't it ironic how so many of us don't attend to numbers while our buyers are fanatically fixated on them, every single day?

Great sales pros measure everything they can think of because they recognize how those numbers influence their behavior. When you learn how to track critical data in your sales day you'll gain more focus, better recognize weaknesses and strengths, and more easily identify where to invest your behavior in order to make more money.

Thank you, by the way, to the late, great Peter Drucker for helping the selling world to recognize the value of this data. This is critical.

If you can't measure it, you can't manage it.

I recall a discussion with my dear friend Gerhard Gschwandtner, founder and publisher of *Selling Power* magazine. I mentioned to him that I'd just done a presentation at a major global training conference where I addressed what's missing from existing sales training.

My seventh of twenty-four points was this observation: *Why don't we give personal budgeting skills training to sales reps?* Their incomes fluctuate as wildly as John Travolta's acting career, so why not help them during the tough times when income dips, so they don't get stressed out, blame the job, and quit or do something dumb, like go deeper into debt?

Gerhard said, "That's interesting you mention that. One of my award-winning sales forces [his magazine annually recognizes bestselling teams] is Shaw Industries. It's the only organization I know that does this type of training."

There are more numbers to consider than just the amount of the commission you make on a sale. Every sales pro should be tracking personal data such as:

‣ *Prospecting Activities.* Which prospects are worthwhile and which are worthless?

   – How quickly did you qualify or disqualify each prospect (to move forward or move on)?

‣ *Phone Activities.* How many phone calls do you make per week?

   – On what percentage of calls did you reach decision makers?

   – Which decision makers agreed to appointments?

‣ *Appointments.* How many face-to-face (or phone) appointments do you schedule per week?

‣ *Objections.* What are your top six objections, and how often does each objection show up? Teams I train always keep track of objections that stop progress in a sale. Using the Ultimate Objection-Handling Tool (Chapter 12), you can adapt these strategies immediately to reduce resistance from buyers.

- *Closing Ratio.* What percentage of your calls gets you not just to the finish line, but in first place as well?

- *Personal Targeted Earnings for the Year.* How much do you want to make (regardless of company expectations)?

- *Incentive to Hit Your Numbers.* That is, what is the value/cost of your personal goal/reward? In other words, do you want a new car? Which one? How much does it cost?

KEY TIP: How much can you live on during dips in your cash flow? Managing your numbers at home—that is, having a personal budget—is critical. In fact, aside from the benefits of managing your home life better, anybody with aspirations to sales management, or even entrepreneurship, has to be able to manage money (or, minimally, marry someone who can). Okay, that last comment is only half true because while you can count on others, there are some things about which you need to have some basic knowledge, too, so that you can advance your professional skills. And aren't you in the business of helping buyers manage their money? When you have the savvy to help quantify buying decisions, you'll persuade more prospects to say yes.

Here's the exercise I teach to help sales pros understand exactly what numbers can influence behavior change and skill improvement. You take your targeted earnings and work backward to identify individual selling activities needed to attain your goal.

How to Start at the Finish Line and Back Up to End Up a Winner

With the idea in mind that time management is founded in goal setting, you'll want to develop the disciplined behavior that extraordinary earners practice every day to make great money. Regardless of what level of experience you've achieved in your sales career, implement these three steps immediately:

1. Define and write down what goal you want to acquire.

2. Set a time frame for acquiring your goal.

3. Pretend you've already gotten your hands on that goal; then *work backward* to determine what activities it would take to attain it.

In social psychology this strategy is called "future pacing." You set your future in place and monitor behavior changes that meet that goal down the road.

Here's a simple example of how to work backward to identify your success path. You can play with the numbers and see how small changes can have a huge impact on final earnings.

BUILD A SPREADSHEET!

Your goal is to pay cash for a new Infiniti automobile, which costs $60,000. You want to be driving it within one year. Follow these steps to create a professional plan for your daily work activities; the bolded words are fields to match with the accompanying spreadsheet:

- You want $60,000 to buy your new Infiniti—in one year. **GOAL**

- You make a $500 commission for each sale. **Com$**

- You need 120 sales to award yourself the car. **SlsYr**

- This means you need ten sales each month. **SlsMo**

- You close 20 percent of your face-to-face sales calls. **ClsF2F**

- At that close rate, you need to get in front of fifty buyers a month to close those ten sales. **TotF2F**

- You have twenty-five workdays each month, so you need two sales calls per day. **DaysMo and ClsDay**

- If you get appointments with one of four phone contacts, you need to contact 200 people (**CntNo**) to get your fifty appointments. **APPT%**

- You need eight daily phone contacts (200 ÷ 25 = 8). **ConDay**

- For every twenty calls you make, you get eight contacts. **TotCall**

▶ Result: You need twenty phone calls and two meetings each day to meet your goal and earn your $60,000 car. **DayAct**

All this activity drives your regular behavior on the job. By employing these guidelines you develop a professional attack on your marketplace.

The accompanying spreadsheet is populated with data from this example. You can, however, work through these steps with your own figures to determine your daily activity. You'll be perceived as a pro. You'll feel like a pro. And you'll pay yourself like a pro.

FIELD	DESCRIPTION	FIGURE
Goal	Dollar amount of your goal	$60,000
Com$	Commission earned per sale	$500
SlsYr	Sales needed per year to meet your goal	120
SlsMo	Sales needed per month to meet your goal	10
ClsF2F	Percentage of face-to-face sales calls you close	20%
TotF2F	Number of sales calls needed to meet sales goal for the month	50
DaysMo	Days worked per month	25
ClsDay	Sales calls needed per day worked	2
Appt%	Percentage of phone contacts that result in an appointment	25%
CntNo	Number of contacts needed to meet appointment goal	200
ConDay	Number of contacts needed per day worked	8
Call%	Percentage of phone calls that result in a contact	40%
CallNo	Number of phone calls needed per day worked	20

▶ ▶ ▶

Create your own spreadsheet, or have your sales pros hand out and work through the example provided in this chapter. When salespeople create their planning and goal-setting numbers and activities, they own the results and the activities required to attain those results. Understanding the relationship between your goals and how it is defined by daily activity is critical to sales success!

Influence yourself by knowing your numbers and adjusting your behavior to improve performance. All true sales pros know their numbers.

NOTES

1. "Frequent-Flyer Miles: In Terminal Decline?" *Economist,* January 6, 2005.

PART THREE

Implementing Your Influence

The god of many business professionals is known by the name of *lifelong learning*.

Is he good or evil?

Good news and bad news: Being a lifelong learner can be a great thing. You fill your head with the best ideas that help you improve. Impress your friends! Mesmerize your peers! Have a conversation about applying some of these influence strategies and the links among selling, decision making, emotion, and the reptilian brain. Even more good news: You can have regular enriching, uplifting experiences through books, audio programs, videos, and live or web-based training.

The bad news is that most lifelong learners rarely put their learning into action.

Brain clutter isn't much different from office clutter. We spend a lot of time and energy piling it up, but how do we turn it into (and this is the bottom line) money?

The chapters in Part 3 hold some answers. I'll quickly cover:

▶ A summary of strategies

- Information to help you know which of these ideas are most important (e.g., How do I put all these strategies into play? Where do I start? Better yet, what information is most important if I can't get to using all of it?)

- First steps to building these strategies into your training

- How to get a free influence assessment for sales teams

- Tips for how to measure styles of influence for hiring (and personal use)

- Model of Sales Excellence, which is the best assessment for sales professionals in existence. It's based on current research and newer than anything on the market—DiSC, Myers Briggs, etc. You can experience this tool with a free assessment for sales executives who oversee large teams.

Get ready to have a great impact on your organization as you identify your first steps to building new learning into your organization.

CHAPTER 22

A Summary of Strategies

YOUR CHEAT SHEET . . . The information imparted here is geared toward your sales life. Remember, though, that these organic language practices can be used in your personal life as well.

Pattern Interrupt

When sellers refuse to respond in a normal, predictable fashion to buyer resistance, they open that buyer's brain to new possibilities and solutions. This strategy is most useful during objection-handling conversations.

To and Away

Sellers should learn to identify whether buyers are motivated by goals and good things or by problems and pain. It is very important to discover this information very early in the sales process. It affects how the salesperson frames her dialogue.

Proactive and Reactive

Buyers tend to either rush forward and make decisions, or move slowly, gathering data (and frustrating sales pros who want to get down to business). Know which type of buyer you are dealing with and you can change your language choices to accommodate either type.

Internal and External

Some buyers are influenced by their own judgments and experience. Others by outside evidence, testimonials, peer pressure. Recognize this difference early, because it could affect how you converse and whether you share marketing materials, which can best persuade external decision makers.

Options and Procedures

Does your buyer like to follow a systematic approach to making decisions? Or would that person prefer to wing it, be creative? Recognize this trait early, too, because it helps you frame your solution to match the buyer's preference.

General and Specific

Big picture, little pieces? Buyers tend toward a high view of the issues, or else every minute element needs to be attended to. You want to know the buyer's preference and view of the world, because it significantly affects how your dialogue is crafted during the sales process.

Convincer Strategy

This is huge. What does it take for buyers to be convinced that they are okay with your solution? Their four choices include absorbing information visually, by what they hear, by feeling, and by reading. It is also important to understand how often or over what period of time your buyers need this information before they are ready to say *yes*.

Critical Language Tips

Minimizers reduce the value of words that follow. Examples are words like *just* or *only*.

But negates the value of words that precede it. Be careful using this word during any sales conversation, as it can really ruffle feathers.

Might is a word we prefer sellers avoid, because it's "spineless." Believe in what you sell and how your solutions help buyers. Don't show weakness in influence by using weak words.

Presuppositions are words that can unconsciously reference beliefs, often without meaning to do so. *If* and *when* are the most common examples used to identify the seller's beliefs about the future. Do you let it happen (*if*)? Or do you plan for positive results (*when*)?

Euphemisms are safe words that buyers use to hide information. Breaking down these ambiguous words and phrases is a key to outstanding objection-handling skills.

Why is a challenge to the other person's intelligence. Avoid this word and frame questions using *how* instead. To ask *how* is to request information about the process involved in the other person's decision.

Mind-reading occurs when people believe they understand the other person's beliefs or feelings. Don't assume. Ask for a clear picture or verbal clarification of someone's position.

Emotions

Master salespeople know how to evoke emotion. There are forty-eight basic emotions. Understanding whether to use the twenty-four positive emotions or the twenty-four negative ones is related to whether your buyer is motivated toward benefits or away from problems (To and Away).

Storytelling

Stories are the backbone of life itself. Every buyer and every salesperson is writing a story every day. Great sales pros intentionally share stories (with significant emotional context) that help buyers to recognize the value of the seller's solutions.

Questions

Questions move a sales conversation down specific paths toward a close. All sales pros should have five power questions they want answered to advance a sale toward a happy ending.

Objection Handling

Every organization should identify the top six objections encountered during sales calls. Next, the organization can apply three unique strategies to procuring potent responses to these deal killers. Those strategies are:

▸ Brainstorm a power play of responses.

▸ Break down language inside the objection.

▸ Dig deeper.

Listening Skills

Too many business relationships revolve around poor listening practices. Great listeners are patient; listen for emotion; and, most important, have insatiable curiosity about other people and their situation.

The Opening Strategy

A psychologically sound opening dialogue helps a seller take charge of the sales call. This strategy extends to setting expectations about meeting time, establishing an honest dialogue, and identifying specific outcomes for the meeting.

Humor

Humor is undeniably an attractor between human beings. Salespeople can adopt some simple practices in print, on the phone, or in person that can help generate a better connection between buyer and seller.

Potent Communication Skills

These skills help us better connect with others. They help buyers perceive sellers are true professionals. These skills cover verbal, written, and listening abilities.

Cold-Calling Technique

Sales professionals must distinguish themselves from the competition. A unique approach to initial conversations can help do that and advance the initial contact into a true sales opportunity. Instead of a weak, ordinary opening, salespeople must offer a choice of problems they solve for existing clients.

Influencing Your Brain

Healthy mental mindsets, such as strong self-talk, are rarely addressed in sales training. These best practices include dealing with rejection, building resilience, creating and attaining goals, managing and organizing priorities, building balance in one's life, and having a healthy attitude.

Influencing Your Body

Healthy bodies create energy and longevity. Sales pros can attend to good practices for rest and recovery, as well as smart eating habits and strong natural health practices.

Knowing Your Numbers

Peter Drucker said, *If you can't measure it, you can't manage it.* Great sales pros know exactly what they need to do every day to make money. They then know how to prioritize behaviors and either increase or reduce those that have an effect on performance.

CHAPTER 23

Can't Decide What's Most Important?

WHICH OF ALL THESE STRATEGIES ARE BEST? There are a lot of fascinating and powerful ideas in this book. About three dozen, when you break them down.

After delivering a keynote, I'm often asked, "Which concepts will make me money the fastest, or have the biggest impact on my selling, or be easiest to adapt?"

Here are the starters, what I consider to be the critical pieces of the influence puzzle. These are the training modules you'd want to have me build into your existing sales training, if you are looking for that shortcut to influence success. Or do it yourself, if you can manage the exercises and follow-on reinforcement. But here are the top 12, in order of importance.

Strategy 1. Objection Handling

As suggested, every company should identify its top six objections and build powerful and persuasive responses that can be adapted by everyone on the team. This, by far, is my most requested solo-consulting workshop. It's great fun to do and you walk away with a script that the company can use for experienced sales pros and for rookies, forever. Simply put, if you get stuck as soon as you encounter buyer resistance, you'll reduce to zero your chances to persuade anyone of anything!

Strategy 2. Critical Language Tips

These are huge, particularly for anyone selling on the phone. Lots of phone work means you are having a ton of conversations and better opportunities to practice good language habits (and avoid the bad ones, like using the word *why*). While I like everyone to be sensitive to these seven verbal pointers, if you are scripting phone sellers, you can make sure these language strategies are built into scripts. Of all the strategies discussed in this book, these tips are also easiest to practice in your personal life, which makes them easier to use at work.

Strategy 3. Knowing Your Numbers

Everybody should know his own numbers. Salespeople have to be able to recognize what to improve (such as getting past certain objections) and how a bump in performance affects personal earnings (give themselves a raise). This strategy really helps you understand which behaviors have the biggest impact on performance.

Strategy 4. Recognizing "To and Away" Buyers

Most sales training focuses too much on benefits-oriented (*To*) selling. Thanks to the innovative Sandler Sales Institute, there is a trend in selling toward finding the buyer's pain (*Away* strategy). Each approach is sometimes right and sometimes wrong. But you can be right all the time when you have the ability to speak the "dialect" of the buyer in front of you. The starting point for persuasion power is recognizing whether to influence using goals and good things vs. focusing on problems your product or service can solve. To that end, the To and Away strategy is a key element to weave into your training.

Strategy 5. The Opening Strategy

This powerful, unique, *psychologically sound* technique for opening your sales meetings will do some amazing things when your team begins to adapt it. Here, you influence by leading, taking charge of a call from the opening dialogue. This technique eliminates stalls and think-it-overs like nothing you've ever used. It gives focus and allows you to gain information from buyers because they agree to share at the very start. It helps you eliminate poor prospects, too, by showing whether the buyer is willing to respect your time and work together with you to figure out how your solutions fit his concerns.

Strategy 6. Listening Skills

We, collectively, in the world of selling are just bad listeners. We know too much. We want to share it. We badly, badly need to become more curious and quieter when we sell. Great influencers often win over people with silence.

Strategy 7. Influencing Your Brain

Self-talk, rejection, attitude, and balance are the four most important pieces of this strategy. You can teach healthy self-talk (which is relevant well beyond handling rejection); do the exercise to build attitude; give your reps a phrase or two to move beyond rejection; and recognize how important balance is in life, both at work and away from the office.

Strategy 8. Evoking Emotions

Just teaching sensitivity to emotional impact is big. But teach your sales pros to evoke emotion with their language choices and watch how buyers get much more engaged in the conversation about your solutions. This technique can be built, as shown in examples throughout the book, into both in-person and print conversations (including proposals).

Strategy 9. Cold-Calling Technique

Again, for those using the phone (or e-mail) a lot, the cold call is an unusual way to communicate with buyers, but the technique presented in this book can yield high influence. It is also a great elevator pitch and opener for most sales calls.

Strategy 10. Convincer Strategy

Although it's a bit trickier to discover how to use this strategy, it is too powerful to ignore. When you can know exactly how a person arrives at the buying decision—when you get the buyer to the stage where she says, "Hey, I'm feeling okay, good, and safe with this decision!"—then you can really close your sales.

Strategy 11. Differentiating Internal from External Buyers

Because we tend to rely a great deal on great marketing materials (external selling), we can miss the opportunity to connect with buyers who are very internal in their decision-making methods. You want to be prepared to offer lots of evidence for your external buyers, while suggesting to internal buyers that they already know everything they need to know to make the best decision for their organization.

Strategy 12. Influencing Your Body

Okay, it's on the list, but most people ignore the real value of good health. Wellness programs abound for a reason. Healthy bodies create energy and longevity. Sales pros attend to good practices for rest and recovery, as well as smart eating habits and strong natural health practices.

▸ ▸ ▸

That's my top 12 list. You might make adjustments to this list based on how strongly you feel about other strategies you've read in this book. Or, you can always just track me down for a conversation and we'll look at what strategies are a best fit for your sales team's needs and how to turn them into new revenue.

CHAPTER 24

First Step, Next Steps

**WHAT KIND OF LEGACY WILL YOU LEAVE TO YOUR ORGANI-
ZATION?** You are probably unfamiliar with the term *anthropodermic
bibliopegy*. It refers to the practice of binding books in human skin.

There are enough of these books around, if you are willing to look for
them. The College of Physicians of Philadelphia has four of them, Harvard
has one, as does Brown University. Evidently, the Cleveland Public Library
even has a copy of the Koran bound this way. That's what you call a pious
believer.

Maybe when I go, I'll have a sales training manual carved out of my . . .
nah, my wife would never approve.

So, how strongly do you feel about improving sales team performance?

Here's help in getting influence training added to your existing sales
training program (or simply creating some add-on modules). First,
though, I have a suggestion for how to really hook other leaders into the

uniqueness and high value these *Secret Language of Influence* concepts bring to the sales training table.

I suggest you offer a short webinar or live training on one of the top 12 topics identified in Chapter 23. For the highest impact, I'd do part of training on the Ultimate Objection-Handling Tool (i.e., breaking down the words inside the objection) or combine the "To and Away" strategy with a couple of the Critical Language Tips.

Let your leaders in on some of these secrets and you'll see the lightbulbs go on overhead. I get to do this for a living and I'm always delighted by the reactions, regardless of the selling system or level of experience on the team.

> *KEY TIP: Nothing in this book competes or conflicts with existing sales training systems. You will find anything you choose to fit into your methodologies will do so quite easily.*

I base my training on one concept: Changed behavior is the *only* outcome of training.

It isn't about learner experience or gaining knowledge or adopting strategies. It's about making sure that, whatever the topic, the sales professionals in the room exhibit a change in behavior that translates into additional sales.

To that end, if you are in training, then you are in the "before and after" business. If there isn't a distinct difference between rep actions before the training experience and after it, then we have failed.

That's blunt. People hate having the word *failure* attached to anything, but I want you to understand that you have to have changed behavior. To implement this changeover, you should understand the Change Formula.

The formula was made famous by Edgar Schein, a professor at MIT Sloan School of Management. He was given the prestigious American Society for Training and Development (ASTD) Lifetime Achievement Award in May 2000. The concept has origins with other professors, particularly David Gleicher, who holds a Ph.D. in economics from Columbia University.

By understanding the pieces that need to be in place for change to occur, you can focus your strategy on addressing each one of them. Let's first understand the formula itself.

The Change Formula

$$C = D \times V \times F > S$$

In other words, people will Change (C) once they:

1. Are aware of their Dissatisfaction (D) or frustration with their current situation.

2. Are given a Vision (V) for what the future could look like.

3. Are offered the First Steps (F) to transition to that vision.

4. Realize that the Dissatisfaction, Vision, and First Steps are greater motivators than their Status Quo (S), or their current situation. Status Quo (S) is often replaced with Resistance (R) to change.

You want change to happen? You want influence training to be accepted in your organization? You have to recognize and outline the existing Dissatisfaction (e.g., are sales lower than expected or planned?), then offer a Vision (e.g., increased revenue, plus better communication, plus smoother response to objections) *and* First Steps (e.g., set a budget for redesign of existing training). Then all three factors must be greater than the Status Quo or Resistance to change.

Do you notice the To and Away concepts at work in this formula? Vision is a benefit, a goal, or an outcome (ideas buyers move toward). Dissatisfaction is a problem or pain (which they move away from).

First Steps is your call to action. Others must make a decision in order to solve their problems and attain goals. This is the action that really gets the momentum moving in the direction of Change.

▸ ▸ ▸

So you have a little homework: Build a case for implementing influence training. I suggest that you formally position this new knowledge by instituting what I call:

The Organization's Use of Healthy and Influential Language Practices

Potent language skills are the most neglected area of any training, whether in leadership, customer service, or sales. With new information available that can help us identify exactly what motivates buyers to make decisions, we can increase revenue by training our sales team in these psychologically sound best practices. This approach blends into an existing sales system that includes phone and face-to-face selling. It could easily be used with customer service support staff as well.

You have acquired many influential language skills just by reading the lessons in this book. But don't just be a learner. Put these practices into play. Try them out at home, with friends, then at the office, then with outside business relationships. I'm here for you when you need a discussion on selling these concepts into other parts of your organization.

CHAPTER 25

Model of Sales Excellence Tool

AND NOW FOR A WEIRD SALES TRAINING EXPERIENCE . . .
I'm working with a client and partway through the morning's meeting I do a "confession session," where reps share their most embarrassing moment.

It's a very funny time. Colleagues who have known one another for a decade or more are shocked to find out some of the stupid things their peers have done in their selling infancy.

We take a break, and as everyone rushes off to eat, drink, phone, or text, the cartoon used to introduce the discussion (pictured here) is still up on the screen.

A woman walks up to me and barks loudly, "I am very offended by that image."

"What? You are?" I'm shocked. Then people start to gather around as they hear the energy in her voice.

"Yes, it is very obvious that that man is looking up her skirt."

"Are you serious?" I say.

"He is looking up her skirt."

Then there's silence as everyone peers closely at the cartoon. Finally, a man says, "But he has no eyes!"

She glares at him and retorts, "He is looking up her skirt, and it is very offensive."

I struggle with whether to make a witty comment or a sarcastic one, and then resign myself to saying, "I'll have to get that guy a male psychologist."

"Wow," I think, "what kind of baggage is this woman bringing into the training?" I've been training for more than twenty-five years and continue to be entertained and, at times, shocked by what's residing in the heads inside the room.

This whole book is about getting into the head of your buyer, so you'll be interested in something new: It's an assessment that determines decision-making patterns in individuals. It is not a personality or abilities test. It doesn't reveal what people *can* do, but rather what they *will* do.

To say that people *can* do something means that they may have measurable abilities to sell well, but they simply choose to put their energy into nonproductive behavior. To *want* to do something means your hires will engage in the most productive behavior possible.

You must hire, manage, and coach sales pros who *want* to do what's necessary to attain personal success. Then you can optimize revenue with maximum productivity from your selling team. And you eliminate a secret struggle many sales executives have—spending too much money training reps they should not be training.

More Sales Aces—How Does That Sound?

You must be able to recruit and staff your team with people whose behavior is equal to the best, instead of resigning yourself to a team of sales professionals ranging from mediocre to great. This is why the Model of Sales Excellence website has been built for you—so that you can actually *measure and model* top reps. You can create a profile from this model, to use during the hiring process, that will keep you focused on candidates who are most closely aligned *with* your premier performers.

The twenty-minute test is based on many of the language tips you've already learned, as well as many more relevant patterns that couldn't be covered in this book. We call these motivational and attitudinal patterns (MAPs), and they can help identify how a person filters past experience and uses it to make decisions.

Imagine the value of all of your sales reps becoming aware of their own personal patterns, based on their experience. Honestly, I freaked out when I completed this assessment because it was scary accurate and showed me things about myself that I recognized immediately as true, even if I'd never before been aware of it.

But wait, there's more!

The benefits of this go way beyond the goodies you'll get in a late-night commercial. Imagine the power of each rep becoming aware of the individual buyer's tendencies to make decisions. This capacity enables your sales pros to adjust their presentations (whether on the phone or face-to-face) in order to maximize speaking in a dialect that matches the buyer's decision-making patterns. You have a quick, multivalue, high-value test that validates the reality of the content in this book.

The Model of Sales Excellence is a powerful tool because it takes influence to a level beyond the reading of this book. If you want to assess, interpret, and coach your sales team with this tool, visit www.ModelofSales Excellence.com. There are several white papers available with greater detail. Senior sales executives can contact me to get themselves assessed for free—in order to experience this amazing tool.

Spend some time at www.ModelofSalesExcellence.com and get your assessment done. You'll be grateful that options exist that can help you model successful hiring, then build a successful selling system to increase rep performance.

Right now, you are holding in your hands a powerful resource that can significantly change how your sales professionals sell. What's the big secret about the *Secret Language of Influence*? It's really no secret at all!

INDEX